U.S. CITIZEN ✔ Yes

INTERACTIVE CITIZENSHIP PREPARATION

RONNA MAGY

THOMSON
HEINLE

Australia Canada Mexico Singapore Spain United Kingdom United States

The publication of *U.S. Citizen* ☑ *Yes* was directed by the members of the Heinle Secondary and Adult ESL Publishing Team:

Editorial Director: Roseanne Mendoza
Senior Production Services Coordinator: Lisa McLaughlin
Market Development Director: Andy Martin

Also participating in the publication of the program were:

Publisher: Stanley Galek
Senior Assistant Editor: Sally Conover
Manufacturing Coordinator: Mary Beth Hennebury
Full Service Design and Production: PC&F, Inc.
Illustration Program: Dave Blanchette and PC&F, Inc.

ISBN: 0-8384-6714-8

Photo Credits:

Cover: Large top star, top, Beth Easter; left and right, Naomi Huerta; top small star, AP/Wide World Photos; left large star, © Jonathan Stark/Heinle & Heinle; center small star, The Bettmann Archive; right large star, © Jonathan Stark/Heinle & Heinle.

Chapter 1: © Richard Laird/FPG, 1; The Bettmann Archive, 3; Naomi Huerta, 5.

Chapter 2: AP/Wide World Photos, 9; AP/Wide World Photos, 11; North Wind Picture Archives, 11; Naomi Huerta, 13.

Chapter 3: The Bettmann Archive, 17; Naomi Huerta, 21.

Chapter 4: AP/Wide World Photos, 25; The Bettmann Archive, 27 left and right; AP Wide World Photos, 28; Naomi Huerta, 29.

Chapter 5: UPI/Bettmann Newsphotos, 35 left; AP/Wide World Photos, 35 right; AP/Wide World Photos, 36; Naomi Huerta, 38.

Chapter 6: The Bettmann Archive, 42; UPI/Bettmann, 44; Beth Easter, 46.

Chapter 7: AP/Wide World Photos, 50 top and bottom; © Fredrik D. Bodin/Stock Boston, 51; AP/Wide World Photos, 53; Wayne Jones, 54.

Chapter 8: Reuters/Bettmann, 58; AP/Wide World Photos, 60; Naomi Huerta, 62

Chapter 9: Naomi Huerta, 69.

Chapter 10: © Bob Daemmrich/StockBoston, 73; Barbara Grover, 75; Beth Easter, 80.

Appendices: Barbara Grover, 91.

U.S. Department of Justice
Immigration and Naturalization Service

OMB #1115-0009
Application for Naturalization

START HERE - Please Type or Print

Part 1.   Information about you.

Family Name	Given Name	Middle Initial

U.S. Mailing Address - Care of

Street Number and Name	Apt. #

City	County

State	ZIP Code

Date of Birth (month/day/year)	Country of Birth

Social Security #	A #

Part 2.   Basis for Eligibility (check one).

a. ☐ I have been a permanent resident for at least five (5) years .

b. ☐ I have been a permanent resident for at least three (3) years and have been married to a United States Citizen for those three years.

c. ☐ I am a permanent resident child of United States citizen parent(s) .

d. ☐ I am applying on the basis of qualifying military service in the Armed Forces of the U.S. and have attached completed Forms N-426 and G-325B

e. ☐ Other. (Please specify section of law) _____

Part 3.   Additional information about you.

Date you became a permanent resident (month/day/year)	Port admitted with an immigrant visa or INS Office where granted adjustment of status.

Citizenship

Name on alien registration card (if different than in Part 1)

Other names used since you became a permanent resident (including maiden name)

Sex ☐ Male ☐ Female	Height	Marital Status: ☐ Single ☐ Married ☐ Divorced ☐ Widowed

Can you speak, read and write English ?   ☐No ☐Yes.

Absences from the U.S.:

Have you been absent from the U.S. since becoming a permanent resident?   ☐ No ☐Yes

If you answered "Yes" , complete the following. Begin with your most recent absence. If you need more room to explain the reason for an absence or to list more trips, continue on separate paper.

Date left U.S.	Date returned	Did absence last 6 months or more?	Destination	Reason for trip
		☐ Yes ☐ No		
		☐ Yes ☐ No		
		☐ Yes ☐ No		
		☐ Yes ☐ No		
		☐ Yes ☐ No		
		☐ Yes ☐ No		

Form N-400 (Rev. 07/17/91)N   **Continued on back.**

Part 4. Information about your residences and employment.

A. List your addresses during the last five (5) years or since you became a permanent resident, whichever is less. Begin with your current address. If you need more space, continue on separate paper:

Street Number and Name, City, State, Country, and Zip Code	Dates (month/day/year)	
	From	To

B. List your employers during the last five (5) years. List your present or most recent employer first. If none, write "None". If you need more space, continue on separate paper.

Employer's Name	Employer's Address	Dates Employed (month/day/year)		Occupation/position
	Street Name and Number - City, State and ZIP Code	From	To	

Part 5. Information about your marital history.

A. Total number of times you have been married _____ . If you are now married, complete the following regarding your husband or wife.

Family name	Given name	Middle initial

Address

Date of birth (month/day/year)	Country of birth	Citizenship
Social Security#	A# (if applicable)	Immigration status (If not a U.S. citizen)

Naturalization (If applicable)
(month/day/year) _____   Place   (City, State) _____

If you have ever previously been married or if your current spouse has been previously married, please provide the following on separate paper: Name of prior spouse, date of marriage, date marriage ended, how marriage ended and immigration status of prior spouse.

Part 6. Information about your children.

B. Total Number of Children _____ . Complete the following information for each of your children. If the child lives with you, state "with me" in the address column; otherwise give city/state/country of child's current residence. If deceased, write "deceased" in the address column. If you need more space, continue on separate paper.

Full name of child	Date of birth	Country of birth	Citizenship	A - Number	Address

Continued on next page

Continued on back

Part 7. Additional eligibility factors.

Please answer each of the following questions. If your answer is **"Yes"**, explain on a separate paper.

1. Are you now, or have you ever been a member of, or in any way connected or associated with the Communist Party, or ever knowingly aided or supported the Communist Party directly, or indirectly through another organization, group or person, or ever advocated, taught, believed in, or knowingly supported or furthered the interests of communism? ☐ Yes ☐ No
2. During the period March 23, 1933 to May 8, 1945, did you serve in, or were you in any way affiliated with, either directly or indirectly, any military unit, paramilitary unit, police unit, self-defense unit, vigilante unit, citizen unit of the Nazi party or SS, government agency or office, extermination camp, concentration camp, prisoner of war camp, prison, labor camp, detention camp or transit camp, under the control or affiliated with:
    a. The Nazi Government of Germany? ☐ Yes ☐ No
    b. Any government in any area occupied by, allied with, or established with the assistance or cooperation of, the Nazi Government of Germany? ☐ Yes ☐ No
3. Have you at any time, anywhere, ever ordered, incited, assisted, or otherwise participated in the persecution of any person because of race, religion, national origin, or political opinion? ☐ Yes ☐ No
4. Have you ever left the United States to avoid being drafted into the U.S. Armed Forces? ☐ Yes ☐ No
5. Have you ever failed to comply with Selective Service laws? ☐ Yes ☐ No
    If you have registered under the Selective Service laws, complete the following information:
        Selective Service Number:_____ Date Registered:_____
    If you registered before 1978, also provide the following:
        Local Board Number:_____ Classification:_____
6. Did you ever apply for exemption from military service because of alienage, conscientious objections or other reasons? ☐ Yes ☐ No
7. Have you ever deserted from the military, air or naval forces of the United States? ☐ Yes ☐ No
8. Since becoming a permanent resident, have you ever failed to file a federal income tax return? ☐ Yes ☐ No
9. Since becoming a permanent resident, have you filed a federal income tax return as a nonresident or failed to file a federal return because you considered yourself to be a nonresident? ☐ Yes ☐ No
10. Are deportation proceedings pending against you, or have you ever been deported, or ordered deported, or have you ever applied for suspension of deportation? ☐ Yes ☐ No
11. Have you ever claimed in writing, or in any way, to be a United States citizen? ☐ Yes ☐ No
12. Have you ever:
    a. been a habitual drunkard? ☐ Yes ☐ No
    b. advocated or practiced polygamy? ☐ Yes ☐ No
    c. been a prostitute or procured anyone for prostitution? ☐ Yes ☐ No
    d. knowingly and for gain helped any alien to enter the U.S. illegally? ☐ Yes ☐ No
    e. been an illicit trafficker in narcotic drugs or marijuana? ☐ Yes ☐ No
    f. received income from illegal gambling? ☐ Yes ☐ No
    g. given false testimony for the purpose of obtaining any immigration benefit? ☐ Yes ☐ No
13. Have you ever been declared legally incompetent or have you ever been confined as a patient in a mental institution? ☐ Yes ☐ No
14. Were you born with, or have you acquired in same way, any title or order of nobility in any foreign State? ☐ Yes ☐ No
15. Have you ever:
    a. knowingly committed any crime for which you have not been arrested? ☐ Yes ☐ No
    b. been arrested, cited, charged, indicted, convicted, fined or imprisoned for breaking or violating any law or ordinance excluding traffic regulations? ☐ Yes ☐ No
(If you answer yes to 15, in your explanation give the following information for each incident or occurrence the **city**, **state**, and **country**, where the offense took place, the **date** and **nature** of the offense, and the **outcome** or **disposition** of the case).

Part 8. Allegiance to the U.S.

If your answer to any of the following questions is **"NO"**, attach a full explanation:
1. Do you believe in the Constitution and form of government of the U.S.? ☐ Yes ☐ No
2. Are you willing to take the full Oath of Allegiance to the U.S.? (see instructions) ☐ Yes ☐ No
3. If the law requires it, are you willing to bear arms on behalf of the U.S.? ☐ Yes ☐ No
4. If the law requires it, are you willing to perform noncombatant services in the Armed Forces of the U.S.? ☐ Yes ☐ No
5. If the law requires it, are you willing to perform work of national importance under civilian direction? ☐ Yes ☐ No

Form N-400 (Rev 07/17/91)N

Continued on back

Part 9. Memberships and organizations.

A. List your present and past membership in or affiliation with every organization, association, fund, foundation, party, club, society, or similar group in the United States or in any other place. Include any military service in this part. If none, write "none". Include the name of organization, location, dates of membership and the nature of the organization. If additional space is needed, use separate paper.

_____

_____

_____

_____

Part 10. Complete only if you checked block " C " in Part 2.

How many of your parents are U.S. citizens? ☐ One ☐ Both (Give the following about one U.S. citizen parent:)

Family Name	Given Name	Middle Name

Address _____

Basis for citizenship:	Relationship to you (check one): ☐ natural parent ☐ adoptive parent
☐ Birth	
☐ Naturalization Cert. No.	☐ parent of child legitimated after birth

If adopted or legitimated after birth, give date of adoption or, legitimation: *(month.day.year)*_____

Does this parent have legal custody of you? ☐ Yes ☐ No

(Attach a copy of relating evidence to establish that you are the child of this U.S. citizen and evidence of this parent's citizenship.)

Part 11. Signature. *(Read the information on penalties in the instructions before completing this section).*

I certify or, if outside the United States, I swear or affirm, under penalty of perjury under the laws of the United States of America that this application, and the evidence submitted with it, is all true and correct. I authorize the release of any information from my records which the Immigration and Naturalization Service needs to determine eligibility for the benefit I am seeking.

Signature _____ **Date** _____

Please Note: If you do not completely fill out this form, or fail to submit required documents listed in the instructions, you may not be found eligible for naturalization and this application may be denied.

Part 12. Signature of person preparing form if other than above. *(Sign below)*

I declare that I prepared this application at the request of the above person and it is based on all information of which I have knowledge.

Signature _____ **Print Your Name** _____ **Date** _____

Firm Name and Address

DO NOT COMPLETE THE FOLLOWING UNTIL INSTRUCTED TO DO SO AT THE INTERVIEW

I swear that I know the contents of this application, and supplemental pages 1 through_____, that the corrections , numbered 1 through_____, were made at my request, and that this amended application, is true to the best of my knowledge and belief.

_____
(Complete and true signature of applicant)

Subscribed and sworn to before me by the applicant.

_____
(Examiner's Signature)   Date

Introduction

U.S. Citizen ☑ ***Yes*** is a text to prepare beginning and intermediate level adult students of Citizenship and English as a Second Language for the naturalization process. The book consists of ten chapters that present the content a student is required to learn to become a citizen of the United States. Activities are developed that encourage students to talk and interact in groups. The book builds on students' life skills and knowledge while encouraging them to compare life in the United States with life in their native countries.

Pages 82 to 92 invite the lower-level student to learn about citizenship. These visually-rich pages familiarize the students with the content in a nonthreatening format so that they can more easily access the naturalization information in the rest of the book.

The first five chapters of the book cover U.S. history: explorers and colonization, the American Revolution and the Declaration of Independence, the Constitution and the Bill of Rights, the 1800s and the Civil War, and the twentieth century. The last five chapters cover the symbols and songs of the United States, the Legislative, Executive, and Judicial Branches, state and local government, and the final interview with the Immigration and Naturalization Service (INS).

In the text, essential information on U.S. history, government, and civics is integrated with the skills of listening, speaking, reading, and writing in English. Every chapter includes a practice test with multiple-choice, dictation, and interview questions to familiarize students with INS testing procedures.

Throughout the book, clarification strategies have been introduced to help students at their interviews. Included in Appendix B are the 100 INS questions and answers. In the front of the book is a copy of the INS N-400 Form (application for citizenship form). Timelines are presented throughout the book to help students sequence and put events into historical context.

Each theme-based chapter begins with lively and interactive prereading activities. Students and their instructor participate actively in these individual, pair, group, and whole-class activities. A class brainstorm of focus words leads students into the content reading. From the reading, students create, review, and expand their personal dictionaries of key vocabulary words. Postreading activities include a comprehension check and a vocabulary review. A role play leads students off the printed page and into historical reality.

Interview questions and personal stories written by other students act as springboards to suggested writing topics. Multiple-choice test questions, INS interview questions, and a dictation, prepare students for their citizenship test. Each chapter ends with a board game that reviews the content of the lesson and encourages interactivity.

Table of Contents

CHAPTER 1

Coming to America

1 ▽ Before You Read

A. Sit in a group of four. Look at the map on the inside cover. Draw a line from your native country to the city where you live now. Do the same for your classmates.

B. Find out about your classmates. Fill in the chart.
1. What's your name?
2. What country are you from?
3. When did you come to the United States?
4. How did you come to the United States? (walk, bus, car, train, boat, plane)

Name	Country	When	How
Elena	El Salvador	1987	plane and car

▼ ▼ ▼ 1

C. Tell your class about one student in your group.

EXAMPLE: Elena is from El Salvador. She came in 1987.
She came to the United States by plane and car.

2 Citizenship Reading

A. What do you know about these words? Write your ideas on the lines.

B. Read

Spanish Exploration: Columbus   Christopher Columbus was an explorer and trader. He was looking for a new way to India. He was looking for spices, silk, and gold. Queen Isabella and King Ferdinand of Spain paid for his trip. Columbus and his crew sailed across the Atlantic Ocean on three ships, the Niña, the Pinta, and the Santa María. In 1492 they landed on an island in the Caribbean Sea. They named the island San Salvador. Because he was looking for India, Columbus named the Native Americans he saw *indios* (Indians). Europeans called the place where Columbus landed the New World.

Other Exploration   In 1519, Hernan Cortés invaded and conquered the Aztec city of Tenochtitlán, now called Mexico City. After Cortés, Spanish explorers, Francisco Vásquez de Coronado and Hernando de Soto, came to what is now New Mexico looking for gold and silver. In 1619, the Spanish built a mission at San Gerónimo, in what is now New Mexico. The Spanish built other missions in California, Texas, and New Mexico. They wanted to convert the native peoples to Christianity.

After Columbus, other explorers from England, France, Holland, Spain, and Portugal traveled to the Americas. Some explorers became rich from the furs, fish, gold, silver, and land they took from the Native Americans. Many colonists forced the Native Americans to work on farms and in mines. Many Native Americans developed serious diseases and died from contact with the explorers. The Native Americans tried to fight against the Europeans, but the Europeans' guns were stronger.

English Settlement at Jamestown Colony   In 1607, English settlers were sent by the Virginia Company to begin a trading post

An Algonquin

Pilgrims

in America. They landed near Chesapeake Bay, Virginia. They established the first English colony at Jamestown, named after King James of England. Winters were very cold in Virginia and the settlers had no food. Sometimes they ate dogs, rats, and mice to survive. Unfortunately, many early Jamestown colonists died of hunger, disease, and cold, but the colony of Jamestown survived.

The Pilgrims at Plymouth Colony   The Pilgrims were part of a religious group that wanted freedom from the Church of England. They left England in 1620 and sailed to North America. They sailed on the ship called the *Mayflower*. The Pilgrims wanted to go to Virginia, instead the *Mayflower* landed at Plymouth, Massachusetts. The weather in the winter of 1620 was very cold and often the Pilgrims had no food. One half of the Pilgrims died that winter. In 1621, the Native Americans taught the Pilgrims how to survive by fishing and hunting, building houses, and planting corn.

After their first harvest in 1621, the Pilgrims celebrated Thanksgiving with the Native Americans. They wanted to thank God for their food and their new lives. Now, we celebrate Thanksgiving on the fourth Thursday in November. On Thanksgiving, some traditional foods we eat are turkey, stuffing, corn, and pumpkin pie.

C. Read the story again. Circle any new words. Begin making your own dictionary of new vocabulary words. Discuss the new words with your teacher and your class.

Columbus lands at San Salvador	Cortés invades Mexico	British colonists settle at Jamestown	Spanish build mission at San Gerónimo (now New Mexico)	Pilgrims settle at Plymouth
1492	1519	1607	1619	1620

▼ ▼ ▼ 3

3 ▽ After You Read

A. Read the sentences. Put a ✔ in the correct column. You may check more than one column.

	Columbus	Pilgrims
1. Who looked for a new route to India?	✔	
2. Who sailed across the Atlantic Ocean?		
3. Who came for religious freedom?		
4. Who was looking for spices, silk, and gold?		
5. Who did the Native Americans teach to plant corn?		

B. Fill in the words. Read the story with a classmate.

landed   Indians   Mayflower   colony
religious freedom   died   Thanksgiving   missions
Pilgrims   ~~India~~

In 1492 Columbus was looking for _____India_____ . His ships,
the Niña, the Pinta, and the Santa María, _____ at San
Salvador Island. Columbus named the Native Americans he met
indios or _____ .

Jamestown was the first English _____ in North
America. Many Jamestown colonists _____ because there
was no food and the weather was cold.

Spanish explorers came to North America in the 1500s. The
Spanish built _____ in California, Texas, and New Mexico.

The _____ came to America from England. They
wanted to have _____ _____ . They sailed on the
_____ . The ship landed at Plymouth, Massachusetts.
Living in a new country was difficult for the Pilgrims. The Native
Americans showed the Pilgrims how to plant corn, hunt, fish and
build houses. In 1621 the Pilgrims and Indians (Native Americans)
celebrated the first _____ .

4 ⟐ Make It Real

A. Sit in a group of four. Read the scenes below. Talk in your group about one scene.

<table>
<tr><td>

SCENE 1

Imagine you are a Native American. You see the Pilgrims arrive at Plymouth, Massachusetts. Talk about how you feel. One group member writes the ideas.

</td><td>

SCENE 2

Imagine you are a Pilgrim. It is the spring of 1621. Many of your people have died. Some Native Americans come to help you. Talk about how you feel. One group member writes the ideas.

</td></tr>
</table>

B. Now, meet a student from the other group. Introduce yourself. Talk about your feelings toward the other group. Talk about your future. Talk about your past.

5 ⟐ Real Stories

A. Read a student's story.

Carlos Reyes

MEMORIES OF A HOMELAND

When I think of El Salvador, I especially miss three things. First, I miss looking at the stars at night. I used to pretend to be an astronomer and study the stars. Second, I miss the aroma of the guava trees and roses surrounding my house. I loved when the smells of the roses and the guava trees were so close to the window that I could reach them. Third, I really miss hiking in the mountains that were filled with different kinds of tropical fruits. I could find mango trees and coconut trees in the mountains.

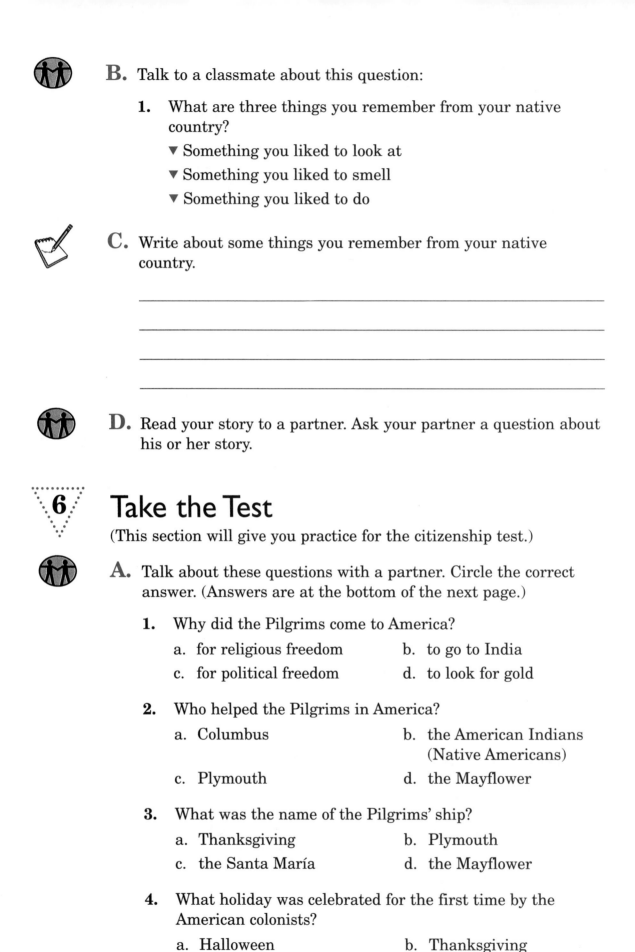

B. Talk to a classmate about this question:

   1. What are three things you remember from your native country?

      ▼ Something you liked to look at

      ▼ Something you liked to smell

      ▼ Something you liked to do

C. Write about some things you remember from your native country.

_____

_____

_____

_____

D. Read your story to a partner. Ask your partner a question about his or her story.

6 Take the Test

(This section will give you practice for the citizenship test.)

A. Talk about these questions with a partner. Circle the correct answer. (Answers are at the bottom of the next page.)

   1. Why did the Pilgrims come to America?

      a. for religious freedom   b. to go to India

      c. for political freedom   d. to look for gold

   2. Who helped the Pilgrims in America?

      a. Columbus   b. the American Indians (Native Americans)

      c. Plymouth   d. the Mayflower

   3. What was the name of the Pilgrims' ship?

      a. Thanksgiving   b. Plymouth

      c. the Santa María   d. the Mayflower

   4. What holiday was celebrated for the first time by the American colonists?

      a. Halloween   b. Thanksgiving

      c. Christmas   d. New Year's Eve

B. Sit with a partner. Student A dictates sentences 1 and 2 to Student B. Student B dictates sentences 3 and 4 to Student A. Check your sentences.

1. I live in the United States of America.

2. My skirt is red.

3. Thanksgiving Day is the fourth Thursday in November.

4. My shirt is blue.

C. Personal Information Questions: Interview a partner. (See page 77 in Chapter 10 for additional questions.)

1. What's your name?
2. What's your address?
3. What's your birthdate?
4. What's your alien registration number?

▼ ▼

D. Clarification: If you don't understand something in the interview, you can say: *I'm sorry. I don't understand your question.*

7 ▽ Think About Your Learning

A. My favorite activity in this unit was _____.

I want to study more about:

▼ Native Americans   ▼ Columbus

▼ Spanish Explorers   ▼ Jamestown Colony

▼ Pilgrims   ▼ _____
                                               (other)

Answers: 1.a 2.b 3.d 4.b

	What year was the first Thanksgiving?	What are traditional Thanksgiving foods?	When is Thanksgiving celebrated in the United States?	**FINISH**
	Who helped the Pilgrims hunt, fish, build houses, and grow corn?	Where did the Mayflower land?	Where did the Pilgrims want to go?	How did the Pilgrims come to America?
What did Europeans call America?	What country did the Pilgrims come from?		What year did the Pilgrims come to America?	Why did the Pilgrims come to America?
	What things was Columbus looking for?	What did Columbus name the Native Americans?	Where did Columbus and his crew land?	What were the names of the ships?
START	Who was Columbus?	What country was Columbus looking for?	Who paid for his trip to America?	

Game instructions are on page 101 of Notes to the User.

The American Revolution and the Declaration of Independence

▽1 Before You Read

A. Sit in a group of four. Look at the picture above. Talk about the questions.

1. Why did you leave your country? (war, no jobs, money, political problems)
2. Who did you leave behind in your country?
3. Why did you decide to come to the United States?

B. Discuss these questions with your group. Write your answers in the chart on the next page.

What are some important things you brought with you from your country?

EXAMPLES: photos, marriage certificate

What are some ideas you brought with you from your country?

EXAMPLES: work hard, save money

Things	Ideas

C. Read your group's list to the class. Listen while the other groups read their lists. Write any new ideas on this page.

2 Citizenship Reading

A. What do you know about these words? Write your ideas on the lines.

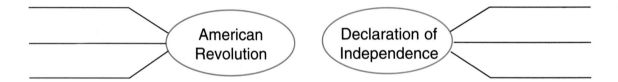

American Revolution

Declaration of Independence

B. Read

Before the Revolution King George III of England controlled the 13 colonies under English law and with English soldiers. The colonists paid taxes on things like tea, stamps, and sugar. When England tried to increase some taxes, the colonists thought it was unfair and became angry. Patrick Henry, a colonial leader, spoke for other colonists when he said, "Give me liberty or give me death!" He wanted the colonies to separate from England.

In 1770, British soldiers killed five colonial leaders in the city of Boston. One of the leaders was Crispus Attucks, a former black slave. This was called the Boston Massacre. In 1773, the English tried to tax the tea that the colonists drank. Some colonists were angry. They went on a ship in Boston Harbor and threw 90,000 pounds of tea into the water. This was called the Boston Tea Party.

The American Revolution Most colonists wanted to separate from England. They needed to have their own government. They started the Revolutionary War against England in 1775. George Washington was commander-in-chief (leader) of the colonial army.

George Washington

The Thirteen Colonies

The war continued for eight years, until 1783. The colonies won the American Revolution. Later, George Washington became the first president of the United States. He is called, the "Father of Our Country."

Declaration of Independence

In 1776, representatives of the 13 colonies met at the Second Continental Congress in Philadelphia, Pennsylvania. They discussed independence from England. On July 4, 1776, colonial representatives adopted the Declaration of Independence. Thomas Jefferson was the main writer of the Declaration of Independence. The Declaration said "All men are created equal." It said that all people have a right to life, liberty, and the pursuit of happiness. These rights cannot be taken away.

Now, we celebrate July 4th of every year as the Independence Day of the United States.

C. Read the story again. Circle any new words. Add these words to your dictionary. Discuss the new words with your teacher and your class.

Boston Massacre	Boston Tea Party	Revolutionary War begins	Declaration of Independence	Revolutionary War ends
1770	1773	1775	1776	1783

▼ ▼ ▼ 11

3 ▽ After You Read

A. Read the information. Put a ✔ under True or False. Talk about your answers with your classmates.

	True	False
1. The English taxed tea, stamps, and sugar.	✔	
2. Most colonists were happy with the English taxes.		
3. George Washington was the main writer of the Declaration of Independence.		
4. Colonial representatives wrote the Declaration of Independence in 1776.		
5. The Declaration of Independence said "all men are created equal."		

B. Fill in the words. Read the story with a classmate.

taxed   1783   Revolutionary War   Declaration of Independence
won   equal   July 4, 1776   tea
free   angry

In 1770 King George III of England controlled the colonies.

England _____taxed_____ the sugar, tea, and stamps of the colonists.

English soldiers guarded the colonies. The colonists were very

_____ . Most colonists wanted to have a _____

and independent country. Some colonists threw a lot of

_____ in Boston Harbor.

The _____ _____ was fought between

England and the American colonists. The war continued from 1775

to _____ . The Americans _____ the

Revolutionary War. The English lost the war.

During the war, colonial representatives met and wrote the

_____ _____ _____ . The Declaration

of Independence says all men are created _____ . Colonial

representatives adopted it on _____ .

4 Make It Real

A. Sit in a group of four. Read the scenes below. Talk in your group about one scene.

SCENE 1

It is 1773. Imagine you are an English soldier in Boston. Your government is taxing the colonists. You are guarding the colonies for King George III. The colonists are very angry. Talk about how you feel. One group member writes the ideas.

SCENE 2

It is 1776. Imagine you are a colonial representative to the Second Continental Congress in Philadelphia, Pennsylvania. You are writing the Declaration of Independence. You think it is necessary to separate from England. Talk about how you feel. One group member writes the ideas.

B. Now, meet a student from the other group. Introduce yourself. Talk about your feelings toward the other group. Talk about the United States. Talk about the future.

5 Real Stories

A. Read a student's story.

Consuelo Cuellar

ABOUT MY LIFE

My name is Consuelo Cuellar and I was born in Durango, Mexico. In 1984 I came to the United States. I went to school to learn English as a Second Language. I worked at the same time. Then, I got married. So far, I have three children and I am very proud of them. I'm going to work very hard to encourage them to be respectable people. My goals are to get my high school diploma and to continue in college. I want to become a citizen so I can vote and exercise my rights.

B. Talk to a classmate about these questions:

    1. Where were you born?

    2. Why did you come to the United States?

    3. What are some things and ideas you brought with you from your country?

    4. What are your future plans?

 C. Write about your life in the United States.

_____

_____

_____

_____

_____

 D. Read your story to a partner. Ask your partner a question about her or his story.

6 Take the Test

(This section will give you practice for the citizenship test.)

 A. Talk about these questions with a partner. Circle the correct answer. (Answers are at the bottom of the next page.)

    1. Who was the main writer of the Declaration of Independence?

        a. George Washington   b. Thomas Jefferson

        c. Patrick Henry   d. King George III

    2. When was the Declaration of Independence adopted?

        a. 1770   b. 1675

        c. 1783   d. 1776

    3. Who said, "Give me liberty or give me death"?

        a. Thomas Jefferson   b. George Washington

        c. Patrick Henry   d. King George III

    4. Which president is called the "Father of Our Country"?

        a. Abraham Lincoln   b. George Washington

        c. John Adams   d. Alexander Hamilton

B. Sit with a partner. Student A dictates sentences 1 and 2 to Student B. Student B dictates sentences 3 and 4 to Student A. Check your sentences.

1. July 4 is Independence Day.
2. Today is a beautiful day.
3. George Washington was the first president.
4. There were 13 colonies.

C. Eligibility Questions: Interview a partner. (See page 77 in Chapter 10 for additional questions.)

1. How long have you been a permanent resident?
2. When did you enter the United States?
3. Can you speak, read, write, and understand English?
4. Have you ever been absent from the United States since you became a permanent resident?

▼ ▼

D. Clarification: If you don't understand something in the interview, you can say: *Could you please say that again?*

7 Think About Your Learning

A. My favorite activity in this unit was _____.

I want to study more about:

▼ Before the American Revolution   ▼ The Revolutionary War

▼ The Declaration of Independence   ▼ _____
                                                             (other)

Answers: 1. b 2. d 3. c 4. b

	When was the Declaration of Independence signed?	What holiday is celebrated on July 4th?	What day is Independence Day?	**FINISH**
Who was the main writer of the Declaration of Independence?	What is the main idea of the Declaration of Independence?	Who is called "the Father of Our Country"?	Which country won the Revolutionary War?	
When did the Revolutionary War begin?	Which two countries fought in the Revolutionary War?		Who was the commander of the U.S. military?	When did the Revolutionary War end?
	Why did the colonists fight in the Revolutionary War?	What happened at the Boston Tea Party?	Who was killed at the Boston Massacre?	Who said, "Give me liberty or give me death"?
START	Who was the King of England in 1770?	What are three things the English taxed?	What did the colonists think about the taxes?	

CHAPTER 3

The Constitution, the Bill of Rights, and the Amendments

1 ▽ Before You Read

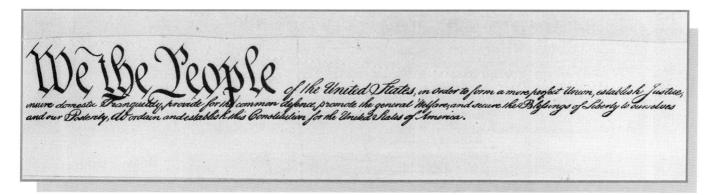

We the People of the United States, in order to form a more perfect Union, establish Justice, insure domestic Tranquility, provide for the common defence, promote the general Welfare, and secure the Blessings of Liberty to ourselves and our Posterity, do ordain and establish this Constitution for the United States of America.

A. Look at the picture above. Ask your partner these questions.

1. Who is the leader of your native country? A president, a king or queen, a military leader, or a religious person?

2. Is the government elected, appointed, or led by the military or a royal family?

3. Who makes the laws in your native country?

4. Did you vote in your native country? Why or why not?

B. Sit in a group of four. Talk about this question. Write your answers in the chart on the next page.

What are some laws of the United States government?

EXAMPLE: You can vote at 18.

Laws of the United States

C. Read your answers to the class.

2 Citizenship Reading

A. What do you know about these words? Write your ideas on the lines.

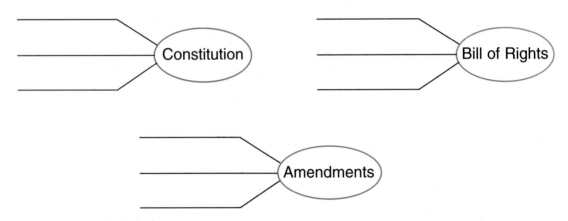

Constitution

Bill of Rights

Amendments

B. Read

The Constitution   After the Revolutionary War, colonial leaders needed to organize a national government. In 1787 they met at the Constitutional Convention in Philadelphia, Pennsylvania. They wanted to protect their rights to freedom and equality. They wrote the United States Constitution.

The Constitution is the plan of government. It explains the government's responsibilities. It is the highest law of the land. The government can pass laws, collect taxes, print money, and organize an army. The Constitution establishes a representative democracy (a republic) as our form of government. It guarantees the rights of all people in the United States, citizens and noncitizens.

There are three branches of government: the executive branch, the legislative branch, and the judicial branch. Some powers are

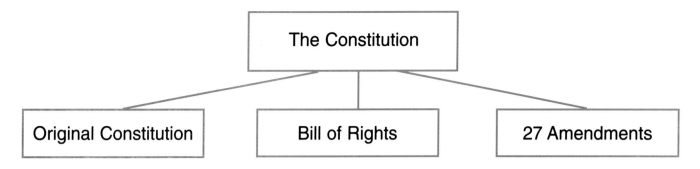

given to the national government, and some powers are given to the states. The Preamble is the beginning of (introduction to) the Constitution.

The Bill of Rights   The Constitution can be changed by the people. A change is called an amendment. The first 10 amendments are called the Bill of Rights. They were adopted in 1791. The First Amendment guarantees freedom of speech, freedom of the press, freedom of religion, the right to assemble (hold a meeting), and the right to ask for a change of government. Some other amendments in the Bill of Rights guarantee the rights of people accused of crimes. For example: A person accused of a crime has a right to have a lawyer and the right to a trial by jury.

The Amendments   Today, there are 27 amendments to the Constitution. The Thirteenth Amendment freed the slaves. It passed in 1865. The Fifteenth Amendment guaranteed the slaves the right to vote. It passed in 1870. The Nineteenth Amendment guaranteed women's right to vote. It passed in 1920. The Twenty-sixth Amendment to the Constitution established the minimum voting age at 18. It passed in 1971. The right to vote is the most important right of a U. S. citizen. Amendments Fifteen, Nineteen, Twenty-four, and Twenty-six guarantee citizens the right to vote.

C. Read the story again. Circle any new words. Add these words to your dictionary. Discuss the new words with your teacher and your class.

Revolutionary War ends

Constitution writ-
ten

Bill of Rights
adopted

Thirteenth
Amendment

Fifteenth
Amendment

Nineteenth
Amendment

Twenty-sixth
Amendment

| 1783 | 1787 | 1791 | 1865 | 1870 | 1920 | 1971 |

3 ▽ After You Read

A. Read the sentences. Put a ✔ under True or False.

	True	False
1. A change to the Constitution is an amendment.	✔	
2. There are 30 amendments to the Constitution.		
3. The Bill of Rights is the first ten amendments.		
4. The Constitution was written in 1787.		
5. The form of government in the United States is a republic.		

B. Fill in the words. Read the story with a classmate.

amendments	Bill of Rights	18	twenty-sixth
~~Constitution~~	Philadelphia	vote	27
freedom of speech, religion, press, assembly	noncitizens		

The U. S. _Constitution_ was written in 1787. The
Constitutional Convention was held in _____. The
_____ _____ _____ is another name
for the first ten _____ to the Constitution. An amendment
is a change to the Constitution. Now, there are _____
amendments to the Constitution. The right to _____ is the
most important right guaranteed in the Constitution. A citizen must
be _____ years old to vote. Voting rights are guaranteed in
the fifteenth, nineteenth, twenty-fourth, and _____
amendments.

The Bill of Rights was adopted in 1791. The first amendment in
the Bill of Rights guarantees _____ _____
_____ , _____ , _____ and
_____ . The rights of citizens and _____ are
guaranteed by the Bill of Rights and the Constitution.

4 Make It Real

A. Sit in a group of four. Read the scenes below. Talk in your group about one scene.

SCENE 1	SCENE 2
It is 1787. It is the time of the Constitutional Convention in Philadelphia. Your group opposes having a single president. You think a president is the same as a king. You are afraid one rich man will control the new government. Talk about how you feel. One group member writes the ideas.	It is 1787. It is the time of the Constitutional Convention in Philadelphia. Your group favors having an elected president. You think one person can represent all the people. You think a single president will be the best leader. Talk about how you feel. One group member writes the ideas.

B. Now, meet a student from the other group. Introduce yourself. Talk about your feelings toward the other group. Talk about who will lead the United States.

5 Real Stories

A. Read a student's story.

Eun Jhee

EDUCATION

The reason my family emigrated to the United States was so that my brothers and I could get a better education. In Korea, opportunities to get a higher education are very limited. It reflects badly on your family if you do not get accepted into college, even if you study hard. Mothers get up at four o'clock in the morning to save seats for their children in the library.

There are so many different ways to get a higher education in the United States. You can go to technical school, junior college, college, or university. I personally have received loans from the government so I can continue my studies in school. Now I am studying to be a physical therapist. I have been in college for six years. In one more year I will complete my Master's Degree.

B. Talk to a classmate about this question:

Do you think Eun Jhee could have said this in her own country? Talk about the education system in your country.

C. Write a story about having freedom of speech in the United States.

_____

_____

_____

_____

_____

D. Read your story to a partner. Ask your partner a question about his or her story.

6 Take the Test

(This section will give you practice for the citizenship test.)

A. Talk about these questions with a partner. Circle the correct answer. (Answers are at the bottom of the next page.)

1. What is the supreme law of the United States?
   a. the Constitution
   b. the Declaration of Independence
   c. the Pledge of Allegiance
   d. the Star-Spangled Banner

2. In what year was the Constitution written?
   a. 1607
   b. 1787
   c. 1720
   d. 1492

3. What is the introduction to the Constitution called?
   a. the Bill of Rights
   b. the supreme law of the land
   c. the Preamble
   d. the Declaration of Independence

4. What do we call a change to the Constitution?
   a. a citizen
   b. a representative
   c. an amendment
   d. a report

B. Sit with a partner. Student A dictates sentences 1 and 2 to Student B. Then, Student B dictates sentences 3 and 4 to Student A. Check your sentences.

1. We have freedom of speech in the United States.
2. You must be a U.S. citizen to vote.
3. There are 27 amendments to the Constitution.
4. The Constitution is the highest law of the land.

C. Residence and Employment Questions: Interview a partner. (See page 77 in Chapter 10 for additional questions.)

1. How long have you lived at your present address?
2. How long have you worked at your present job?
3. Why did you leave your last job?
4. Are you receiving welfare or any government assistance?

▼ ▼

D. **Clarification:** If you don't understand something in the interview, you can say: *Could you please repeat that?*

7 Think About Your Learning

A. My favorite activity in this unit was _____.

I want to study more about:

▼ The Constitution   ▼ The Bill of Rights

▼ The Amendments   ▼ _____
   to the Constiutution   *(other)*

Answers: 1.a 2.b 3.c 4.c

▼ ▼ ▼ **23**

	What is the minimum voting age?	What is one amendment that guarantees voting rights?	When was the Nineteenth Amendment passed?	**FINISH**
What is the most important right of U.S. citizens?	What are other rights guaranteed by the Bill of Rights?	What is one right guaranteed by the First Amendment?	Whose rights are guaranteed by the Constitution?	
What is the introduction to the Constitution called?	Which amendment freed the slaves?		Which amendment guaranteed women's right to vote?	When was the Twenty-sixth Amendment passed?
	What is the Bill of Rights?	What kind of government does the United States have?	What are the three branches of government?	How many amendments are there to the Constitution?
START	What is the Constitution?	When was the Constitution written?	What do we call a change to the Constitution?	

CHAPTER 4

Growth and the Civil War

1 ▽ Before You Read

A. Talk about these questions with a partner.

1. Are there political problems or economic problems in your native country?
2. Was there a war there? When?
3. What is or was the reason for the problems?
4. What is or was a way to stop the problems?

B. Sit in a group of four. Find out about your classmates. Fill in the chart.

1. What's your name?
2. Where were you born?
3. Is there a war in your native country?
4. What are your native country's problems?

Name	Country	War	Problems
Isabel	Italy	no	not enough jobs

C. Tell your class about one student in your group.

EXAMPLE: Isabel was born in Italy. There is no war now. The people need more jobs.

2 ▽ Citizenship Reading

A. What do you know about these words? Write your ideas on the lines.

Slavery

Freedom

B. Read.

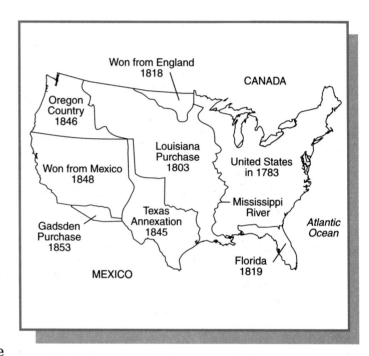

Won from England
1818

CANADA

Oregon
Country
1846

Louisiana
Purchase
1803

United States
in 1783

Won from Mexico
1848

Mississippi
River

Atlantic
Ocean

Texas
Annexation
1845

Gadsden
Purchase
1853

Florida
1819

MEXICO

The United States Grows
In 1775 there were 13 colonies in the United States. Between 1800 and 1853 the country expanded west to the Pacific Ocean. The United States acquired lands from England, France, Spain, and Mexico. Originally, all these lands belonged to the Native Americans.

The population increased. Many people moved to the South and West of the United States. After 1840, many new immigrants came from Europe and Asia. They wanted freedom, land, and better jobs. The United States government forced the Native Americans off their own lands and gave the lands to settlers.

Slave or Free From the 1600s to the 1800s people from different areas of Africa were forced to come to the United States as slaves. They were brought by slave traders. In Africa, they were free. They were bought and sold in the United States. Many worked on plantations (large farms) in the South. Some escaped to freedom in the North on the Underground Railroad. The Underground Railroad was organized by people opposed to slavery. It helped slaves escape to freedom.

Separate cultures developed in the North and in the South. About one fourth of Southern people were large plantation owners. The others were small farmers. The economy of the South depended on farming cotton and slavery. The people in the South believed in the rights of the individual states and in a small federal government. The economy of the North depended on industry and the growth of

Sojourner Truth, a northern slave who was freed. She fought for the rights of slaves and women

Abraham Lincoln, sixteenth president

cities. Factory workers in the North made shoes, clothing, guns, and tools. Many people in the North were against the expansion of slavery into new states and territories.

The Civil War and President Lincoln

The northern and southern states were divided on the issue of slavery. Between 1861 and 1865 the North (the Union) and the South (the Confederacy) fought the Civil War. The South seceded (separated) from the Union and the first shot of the war was fired. More than 600,000 soldiers died in that war.

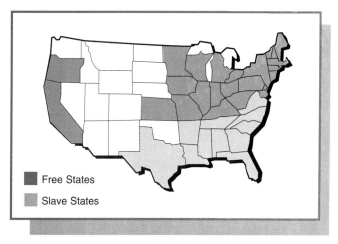

Free States
Slave States

Abraham Lincoln was elected the sixteenth president in 1861. Lincoln was president during the Civil War. He wanted to keep the North and the South together as one nation. He did not want the Union to be divided. On January 1, 1863, Lincoln signed the Emancipation Proclamation. The Emancipation Proclamation freed the slaves.

On April 9, 1865, the North won the Civil War. The Thirteenth Amendment was passed in 1865. It ended slavery. Lincoln was assassinated on April 14, 1865. Americans remember Lincoln because he united the country and freed the slaves. His birthday on February 12 is a national holiday.

C. Read the story again. Circle any new words. Add these words to your dictionary. Discuss the new words with your teacher and your class.

United States expands territory	Civil War begins	Emancipation Proclamation issued	Civil War ends	Lincoln assassinated	Thirteenth Amendment adopted
1800–1853	July, 1861	Jan. 1, 1863	April 9, 1865	April 14, 1865	1865

3 After You Read

A. Fill in the words. Read and compare the sentences with a classmate.

1. a. The American Revolution began in 1778.
   b. The Civil War began in _____.

2. a. In the Revolutionary War, the colonists fought against the English.
   b. In the Civil War, the _____ fought against the _____.

3. a. George Washington was the president after the American Revolution.
   b. _____ _____ was the president during the Civil War.

4. a. Colonial representatives signed the Declaration of Independence.
   b. Abraham Lincoln signed the _____ _____.

B. Fill in the words. Read the story with a classmate.

slaves	~~expanded~~	free
North	South	immigrants
won	Civil	Emancipation Proclamation

Between 1800 and 1853, the United States __expanded__ to the west. After 1840, many new _____ came from countries in Europe and Asia.

African _____ worked on plantations in the South. The slaves were not _____. The states of the _____ wanted workers to be free. The states of the _____ wanted to have slaves.

The _____ War was fought between 1861 and 1865. Abraham Lincoln was the president. The North _____ the war. In 1863 Lincoln signed the _____ _____. It freed the slaves.

Frederick Douglass
African-American anti-slavery leader

4 Make It Real

A. Sit in a group of four. Read the scenes below. Talk in your group about one scene.

SCENE 1 It is 1850. You are an African slave forced to come to America. You live on a Southern plantation. You want to escape to the North. Talk to the other slaves about why you want to be free. One group member writes the ideas.	**SCENE 2** It is 1850. You are a Southern plantation owner. You are a religious person. You own 100 slaves. You say that God thinks slavery is good for African people. Talk to other plantation owners about how you feel. One group member writes the ideas.

B. Now, meet a student from the other group. Introduce yourself. Talk about your feelings toward the other group. Talk about your past. Talk about slavery. Talk about the plantation. Talk about the future.

5 Real Stories

A. Read a student's story:

Vesna Budincich

LEAVING MY NATIVE COUNTRY

My name is Vesna. I came to Los Angeles from Sarajevo. Formerly it was part of Yugoslavia. Now, it is in Bosnia-Herzegovina. There has been a terrible civil war going on there for four years now. People who used to live in harmony together as we do here in the United States now live with hatred for each other.

My future in my home country is unknown. I have lost my home. My father, who was a civilian, was killed on his way home from work in 1992. My mother and my two sisters are still in Bosnia. I have no job to go back to. I don't want to return to live in that city. I want to stay here and become a citizen of the United States.

B. Talk to a classmate about these questions:

1. How long did you live in your native country?
2. What were the political or economic problems in your native country?
3. Why did you leave your country?
4. Who did you leave behind when you came here?

C. Write about why you left your native country and who you left behind.

_____

_____

_____

_____

_____

D. Read your story to a partner. Ask your partner a question about his or her story.

6 ▽ Take the Test

(This section will give you practice for the citizenship test.)

A. Talk about these questions with a partner. Circle the correct answer. (Answers are at the bottom of this page.)

1. Who was the president during the Civil War?
   - a. George Washington
   - b. Thomas Jefferson
   - c. Abraham Lincoln
   - d. Benjamin Franklin

2. What did the Emancipation Proclamation do?
   - a. gave women the vote
   - b. gave freedom of speech
   - c. ended the Civil War
   - d. freed the slaves

3. Which president freed the slaves?
   - a. Abraham Lincoln
   - b. Ronald Reagan
   - c. Jimmy Carter
   - d. George Washington

Answers: 1. c 2. d 3. a

B. Sit with a partner. Student A dictates sentences 1 and 2 to Student B. Then, Student B dictates sentences 3 and 4 to Student A. Check your sentences.

1. Lincoln's birthday is February 12.
2. I love the American people.
3. I drive to work every day.
4. The Constitution says we are all equal in America.

C. Marital History Questions: (See page 78 in Chapter 10 for additional questions.)

1. Are you married now?
2. How many times have you been married?
3. What is the name of your spouse?
4. Is your wife or husband a naturalized citizen?

▼▼▼▼▼▼▼▼▼▼▼▼▼▼▼▼▼▼▼▼▼▼▼▼▼▼▼▼▼▼▼▼▼▼

D. Clarification: If you don't understand something in the interview, you can say: *Could you say that again please?*

7 Think About Your Learning

A. My favorite activity in this unit was _____ .

I want to study more about:

▼ Growth and Immigration   ▼ the Civil War

▼ Abraham Lincoln   ▼ Slavery

▼ _____
   (other)

Game board, START to FINISH.

START

After 1800, the United States expanded _____ to the Pacific Ocean.

After 1840, many new _____ came from Europe and Asia.

_____ were brought to America by slave traders.

The _____ fought against the _____ in the Civil War.

Most people in the North wanted workers to be _____ .

Southern plantation owners wanted _____ to farm the land.

_____ were slaves on Southern plantations.

The _____ Railroad freed some slaves.

_____ was the President during the Civil War.

The Civil War began in _____ .

Lincoln issued the _____ _____ in 1863.

Lincoln was _____ in 1865.

The Civil War ended in _____ .

Over _____ people died in the Civil War.

The Emancipation Proclamation _____ the slaves.

The _____ Amendment ended slavery.

Sojourner Truth fought for the _____ of slaves and women.

Frederick Douglass spoke against _____ .

FINISH

5 Twentieth Century

1 ▽ Before You Read

A. Sit in a group of four. Make a list of things about the United States that are different from your native country.

more cars   _tall buildings_   _____

_____   _____   _____

_____   _____   _____

B. What are some things about your life now that are different from your native country? Answer the questions. Fill in the chart.

	Native Country	United States
1. Time you get up?		
2. Clothes you wear?		
3. Foods you eat?		
4. People you live with?		
5. Your job?		
6. Hours you work?		
7. Time you spend with friends and family?		

C. Talk about this question with your partner.

Is your life easier or more difficult in the United States? Why?

Example: **My life is more difficult because I work longer hours.**

2 ▽ Citizenship Reading

A. What do you know about these words? Write your ideas on the lines.

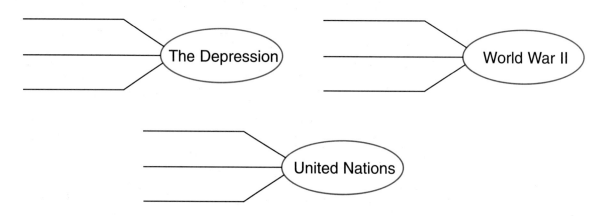

The Depression

World War II

United Nations

B. Read

Industrialization and Labor Factories and machinery were developed in the United States beginning in the mid 1820s. Many people left farms and moved to the cities to find jobs. By the 1920s, more than 50 percent of the U.S. population lived in cities.

Factory workers' lives were difficult in the early 1900s. They worked 10–12 hours a day for very low pay. For the first time their working day was controlled by a time clock. Children worked in the factories. Working conditions were not safe. Some factory owners discriminated against immigrants, non-whites, and women.

Workers fought for and won shorter work days, rest periods, better pay, and safer jobs. Some workers organized into labor unions. The U.S. Congress passed laws restricting child labor. In this same period, women's organizations fought for and won the right for women to vote. This right became law when the Nineteenth Amendment passed in 1920.

World War I World War I, the Great War, began in 1914. The United States tried to stay out of the war. It did not want to be involved in the problems of other countries. In 1917, after Germany bombed U.S. ships, the United States entered the war. England, France, Russia, and the United States were the Allies. The Central Powers: Germany, Austria-Hungary, and Turkey were the enemy. The war was fought over land, power, and money. World War I ended in 1918. The war helped the United States become a world power.

The Great Depression and the New Deal In the 1930s the United States had many economic problems. Businesses and banks were forced to close. People lost their jobs and their savings. Many

Women organized to protest unfair labor practices

Franklin Delano Roosevelt

people lost their homes, had no money, and were hungry. People organized and demanded help from the government.

Franklin Delano Roosevelt was president in 1932. His plan to rebuild the country was called the New Deal. The New Deal created new jobs. People built roads, dams, post offices, and theaters. The government helped some small businesses to get loans. Roosevelt wanted to keep the economy going. Congress passed the Social Security Act and welfare programs. The minimum wage was established for some workers. Roosevelt was president from 1932 to 1945.

World War II   World War II began in 1939. After the Japanese bombed Pearl Harbor on December 7, 1941, the United States entered the war. England, France, Russia, and the United States were the Allies as in World War I. The Axis Powers of Germany, Italy, and Japan were the enemy. Hitler, the dictator of Germany, wanted to control all of Europe. More than 10 million Jews, Catholics, homosexuals, and gypsies were killed by Hitler and the Nazis during the Holocaust.

In August of 1945, the United States dropped atomic bombs on the Japanese cities of Hiroshima and Nagasaki. The war ended in August of 1945. The Allies won World War II.

The United Nations   After World War II, world leaders came together to form the United Nations. They wanted to avoid further conflict. The United Nations (UN) met for the first time in 1946. Countries discuss and try to resolve world problems. The United Nations also gives economic aid (money) to many countries for medical and educational needs.

Vietnam   U.S. soldiers fought in the Vietnam War. The United States sent troops into Vietnam in 1961. Many Americans opposed the war because they didn't think the United States had a good reason to be in Vietnam. Many other Americans supported the war. Finally, in 1973, a peace treaty was signed. Most U.S. soldiers left Vietnam in 1973.

Dr. Martin Luther King, Jr. and Civil Rights

Since the time of slavery, African Americans have fought for civil rights and equal treatment. One civil rights leader was Dr. Martin Luther King, Jr. In his famous speech, "I Have a Dream," he said, "I have a dream that my four little children will one day live in a nation where they will not be judged by the color of their skin, but by the content of their character." He was assassinated in 1968. Dr. Martin Luther King, Jr.'s birthday is a national holiday and is celebrated on the third Monday in January.

Dr. Martin Luther King, Jr.

Asian Americans, Latinos, Native Americans, and people of other nationalities have fought for their civil rights. Women, gays, senior citizens, and disabled groups have fought against discrimination. The fight for equality continues to this day.

C. Read the story again. Circle any new words. Add these words to your dictionary. Discuss the new words with your teacher and your class.

World War I	Nineteenth Amendment	Great Depression begins	New Deal	World War II	First meeting of the United Nations	Vietnam War Era	Dr. Martin Luther King, Jr. Speech
1914–1918	1920	1929	1932	1939–1945	1946	1961–1973	1963

3 After You Read

A. Read the sentences. Put a ✔ under True or False.

		True	False
1.	In the early 1900s, workers fought for shorter work days and better working conditions.	✔	
2.	In the Depression, most people had a lot of food and money.		
3.	In World War II, Germany wanted to control Europe.		
4.	In 1945, the United States dropped bombs on Japan.		
5.	The United Nations met in 1936.		
6.	The Vietnam War was before World War II.		

B. Fill in the words. Read the story with a classmate.

speech   bombs   Dr. Martin Luther King, Jr.   world problems
Russia   1939   Franklin Delano Roosevelt
1918   ~~shorter~~   England

In the early 1900s, workers fought for ____*shorter*____ work

days, better pay, and better working conditions. The United States

was allies with _____, France, and _____ in

World War I. World War I ended in _____. After World

War I, the United States was a world power.

_____ _____ _____ was president

during the 1930s and the Great Depression. World War II began in

_____. In 1945 the United States dropped two atomic

_____ on Japan. After World War II ended, the United

Nations met in 1946 to discuss _____ _____.

_____ _____ _____

_____ , _____ was a famous civil rights leader. He

gave his _____ , "I Have a Dream," in 1963.

4 ▽ Make It Real

A. Sit in a group of four. Read the scenes below. Talk in your group
about one scene.

SCENE 1	SCENE 2
You are a factory worker. You work 10 to 12 hours a day. Your boss refuses to pay you for working overtime. Talk about how you feel. One group member writes the ideas.	You work for the United States Department of Labor. Your job is to make sure workers are paid for overtime work. Talk to the other government workers. What can you do to help the factory worker? One group member writes the ideas.

B. Now, meet a student from the other group. Introduce yourself.
Talk about employee's rights and responsibilities. Talk about
employer's rights and responsibilities.

5 Real Stories

A. Read a student's story

Hava Hava Maim

CHANGES

I grew up in Israel and the people were very close to each other. We knew our neighbors. There was a warm connection between us. People always talked on the street. I felt like I belonged. The doors to our homes were always open.

Moving to the United States was a cultural shock. Learning the language, meeting new people, and learning new social behaviors required a whole new set of rules. One fundamental difference between Israelis and Americans is the way people interact. Americans are much more reserved than Israelis. I think we can learn a lot from each other.

B. Read the story again. Talk to a classmate about this question:

How has Hava's life changed since she came to the United States?

C. Think about Hava's story. Then, look back at the questions on page 33. Write about changes in your life.

_____

_____

_____

_____

_____

D. Read your story to a partner. Ask your partner a question about her or his story.

▽ 6 Take the Test

(This section will give you practice for the citizenship test.)

A. Talk about these questions with a partner. Circle the correct answer. (Answers are at the bottom of this page.)

1. Which countries were our enemies during World War II?
   a. England, France, and Russia
   b. China, Japan, and Korea
   c. England, Spain, and Portugal
   d. Germany, Japan, and Italy

2. Name one purpose of the United Nations.
   a. to discuss and resolve world problems
   b. to review court decisions
   c. to celebrate holidays
   d. to talk about sports events

3. Who was Dr. Martin Luther King, Jr.?
   a. a scientist
   b. a civil rights leader
   c. a famous musician
   d. President of the United States

B. Sit with a partner. Student A dictates sentences 1 and 2 to Student B. Then, Student B dictates sentences 3 and 4 to Student A. Check your sentences.

1. We are all free in the United States.
2. The United Nations met in 1946.
3. I am becoming a citizen of the United States.
4. _____ is the Vice President of the United States.

C. Questions About Children: Interview your partner. (See page 78 in Chapter 10 for additional questions.)

1. What are the names and ages of your children?
2. Where were your children born?
3. What are each of your children's registration numbers?
4. Who supports your children?

▼ ▼

D. Clarification: If you don't understand something in the interview, you can say: *Could you please say that again more slowly?*

Answers: 1. d 2. a 3. b

7 ▽ Think About Your Learning

A. My favorite activity in this unit was _____ .

I want to study more about:

▼ World War I   ▼ the United Nations

▼ the Vietnam War   ▼ Civil Rights

▼ _____
     (other)

When did the Vietnam War end?

Who was Dr. Martin Luther King, Jr.?

On what day is Dr. Martin Luther King, Jr.'s birthday celebrated?

What is Dr. Martin Luther King, Jr.'s famous speech?

FINISH

What does the United Nations do?

What happened in the Holocaust?

Who won World War II?

Who were the Axis powers in World War II?

Who was the President in 1932?

Name three programs that were part of the New Deal.

When did World War II begin?

Who were the Allies in World War II?

Name three things that happened in the Great Depression.

Who were the Central Powers in World War I?

Who were the Allies in World War I?

In what year did World War I end?

START

Name four things workers fought for and won in the early 1900s.

In what year did World War I begin?

Why did the United States want to stay out of World War I?

CHAPTER 6 Celebrations

1 Before You Read

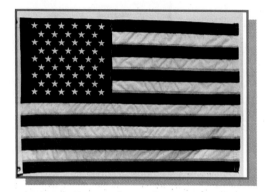  

A. Sit in a group of four. Look at the pictures above. Talk about the questions.

1. When are Flag Day and Independence Day celebrated in the United States?
2. What are some things people do on those days?
3. Are Flag Day and Independence Day celebrated in your native country?
4. What are some things people do?

B. Find out about your classmates. Fill in the chart.

1. What is your name?
2. What country are you from?
3. What are the colors in your country's flag?
4. What symbols are in your country's flag?

Name	Country	Flag Colors	Symbols
Arturo	Mexico	red, white, green	eagle

C. Tell your class about one student in your group.

EXAMPLE: Arturo is from Mexico. His country's flag is red, white, and green. The eagle is the symbol.

2 Citizenship Reading

A. What do you know about these words? Write your ideas on the lines.

The United States Flag

The Star-Spangled Banner

The Pledge of Allegiance

B. Read.

The United States Flag The colors of the United States flag are red, white, and blue. The red means courage, the white means purity, and the blue means justice. The 13 stripes are red and white and represent the original 13 colonies. The 50 white stars represent the 50 states of the United States. Alaska was the 49th state and Hawaii was the 50th state.

The flag became an official national symbol in 1777. Flag Day is celebrated on June 14. On that day many people put a flag in front of their homes, schools, and businesses. Many people feel patriotic on Flag Day.

The Star-Spangled Banner is the national anthem, or song, of the United States. Francis Scott Key wrote the words in 1814. At that time, British soldiers told Francis Scott Key they were going to

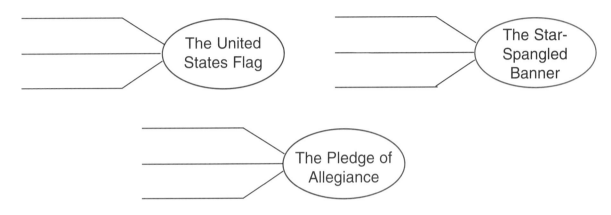

The Star-Spangled Banner

Oh, say, can you see,
    by the dawn's early light,
What so proudly we hailed
    at the twilight's last gleaming.
Whose broad stripes and bright stars,
    through the perilous fight,
O'er the ramparts we watched,
    were so gallantly streaming!
And the rocket's red glare,
    the bombs bursting in air,
Gave proof through the night
    that our flag was still there:
Oh, say, does that star-spangled
    banner yet wave
O'er the land of the free
    and the home of the brave?

The Pledge of Allegiance

I pledge allegiance
to the flag
of the United States of America,
and to the republic
for which it stands,
one nation,
under God,
indivisible,
with liberty
and justice for all.

destroy Fort McHenry and the American flag flying over the fort. They said he would never see that flag again. The next morning the Americans were victorious and Francis Scott Key saw the flag was still flying. He wrote the words to the song.

The United States Congress declared the *Star-Spangled Banner* the national anthem in 1931. People sing the *Star-Spangled Banner* on holidays and at some public ceremonies. Stand and face the flag when you sing the *Star-Spangled Banner*.

The Pledge of Allegiance is a promise by citizens to be loyal to the government of the United States. *The Pledge of Allegiance* says that the Union (the 50 states) cannot be divided. This is one nation and it is indivisible. *The Pledge of Allegiance* says that in the United States there is liberty (freedom) and justice (fairness) for all people. The words, ". . . under God . . ." were added to the *Pledge of Allegiance* in 1954. When you say the *Pledge of Allegiance*, stand and face the flag. Put your right hand over your heart.

C. Read the story again. Circle any new words. Add these new words to your student dictionary. Discuss the new words with your teacher and your class.

A national flag is adopted	Frances Scott Key writes the words to the *Star-Spangled Banner*	First time *Pledge of Allegiance* is said	*Star-Spangled Banner* becomes national anthem
1777	1814	1892–1893	1931

3 ▽ After You Read

A. Read the questions. Write the correct letter next to each number.

_b_ 1.	How many stars are in the flag?	a. red, white, and blue
_____ 2.	How many stripes are in the flag?	b. 50
_____ 3.	What colors are in the flag?	c. 13
_____ 4.	What does the red mean?	d. purity
_____ 5.	What does the white mean?	e. courage

B. Read the sentences. Put a ✔ in the correct column. You may check more than one column.

	Pledge	Star-Spangled Banner
1. You put your hand over your heart.	✔	
2. Francis Scott Key wrote the words in 1814.		
3. You sing, "Oh say can you see . . ."		
4. "One nation, under God, indivisible with liberty and justice for all."		
5. You stand up.		

C. Fill in the words. Read the story with a classmate.

republic   ~~stripes~~   stars   anthem   justice
colonies   Star-Spangled Banner   states   Pledge   Flag Day

The American flag is red, white, and blue. It has 13 _____stripes_____

and 50 _____ . The red and white stripes are for the original

13 _____ . The white stars are for the 50 _____ of

the United States. June 14 is _____ _____ . The

_____-_____ _____ is another name for the

flag. Francis Scott Key wrote the national _____ in 1814.

The _____ of Allegiance says we are one nation. "I

pledge allegiance to the flag of the United States of America, and to

the _____ for which it stands, one nation, under God,

indivisible, with liberty and _____ for all."

4 ▽ Make It Real

A. Sit in a group of four. Read the scenes below. Talk in your group about one scene.

SCENE 1

Imagine you are Francis Scott Key. One night you are watching a battle of the War of 1812. When you wake up the next morning, the American flag is still flying. You feel very proud. Talk about how you feel. One group member writes the ideas.

SCENE 2

Imagine you are becoming a citizen of the United States. It is almost 200 years after Francis Scott Key wrote the *Star-Spangled Banner*. You are going to sing the song at your naturalization (citizenship) ceremony. Talk about how you feel. One group member writes the ideas.

B. Now, meet a student from the other group. Introduce yourself. Talk about the United States. Talk about its past and its future. Talk about how things have changed.

5 ▽ Real Stories

A. Read a student's story.

HOW I FEEL WHEN I LOOK AT THE FLAG

When I lived in Russia, I knew which flag the United States of America had, and I knew about its political system. At that time, however, I did not have any feelings for the American flag.

After I had been here for four years, I appreciated the American flag in a new way. I understood that the flag symbolized the American way of life. All 50 states guarantee the same rights for everyone. Every person has these rights regardless of nationality, religion, or social beliefs. The 13 stripes on the American flag represent the original 13 colonies, the foundation for our democratic nation. In this nation there is freedom for everyone.

Victor Dinsburg

B. Talk to a classmate about these questions:

1. Before you came to the United States, how did you feel when you looked at the flag?

2. How do you feel now when you look at the flag?

C. Write about the U.S. flag. You can write about how you feel when you see it, what it represents to you, or any experience you have had with the American flag.

_____

_____

_____

_____

D. Read your story to a partner. Ask your partner a question about her or his story.

6 ▽ Take the Test

(This section will give you practice for the citizenship test.)

A. Talk about these questions with a partner. Circle the correct answer. (Answers are at the bottom of this page.)

1. What are the colors of the American flag?
   a. red, yellow, and green
   b. blue, orange, and yellow
   c. red, white, and blue
   d. green, yellow, and blue

2. What do the stripes in the flag mean?
   a. the original 20 colonies
   b. the original 13 colonies
   c. Alaska and Hawaii
   d. the 50 states

3. What do the stars in the flag mean?
   a. One for each state in the Union
   b. One for each of the 13 colonies
   c. the *Star-Spangled Banner*
   d. the *Pledge of Allegiance*

4. Who wrote the *Star-Spangled Banner*?
   a. Patrick Henry
   b. Thomas Jefferson
   c. George Washington
   d. Francis Scott Key

Answers: 1. c   2. b   3. a   4. d

B. Sit with a partner. Student A dictates sentences 1 and 2 to Student B. Then, Student B dictates sentences 3 and 4 to Student A. Check your sentences.

1. The American flag is red, white, and blue.
2. The United States has fifty (50) states.
3. The American flag has fifty (50) stars.
4. The United States flag has thirteen (13) stripes.

C. More Eligibility Questions: Interview your partner. (See pages 78 and 79 in Chapter 10 for additional questions.)

1. Have you ever been associated with the Communist Party?
2. Were you connected with the Nazi Government of Germany between 1933 and 1945?
3. When did you register with the Selective Service?
4. What is your Selective Service number?

▼ ▼

D. Clarification: If you don't understand something in the interview, you can say: *Could you please say that again more slowly?*

7 Think About Your Learning

A. My favorite activity in this unit was _____ .

I want to study more about:

    ▼ *The Pledge of Allegiance*   ▼ The United States Flag

    ▼ *The Star-Spangled Banner*   ▼ _____
                                                                       (other)

June 14 Flag Day	Who wrote the song, *The Star-Spangled Banner?*	What year did Francis Scott Key write *The Star-Spangled Banner?*	Say *the Pledge of Allegiance.*	**FINISH** 
What is the national anthem of the United States?	How many states are in the United States now?	What day is Flag Day?	What day is Independence Day?	4TH
What does the red in the flag mean?	What does the white in the flag mean?		What does the blue in the flag mean?	What were the first thirteen states called?
THE CONSTITUTION	What are the three colors in the flag?	What colors are the stripes?	What do the stripes mean?	How many stripes are in the flag?
START 	How many stars are in the flag?	What do the stars mean?	What color are the stars?	BALLOT VOTE TODAY

7 The Legislature

 1 ## Before You Read

A. Look at the picture with your class. Talk about the question. Write your answers.

What are the rules in our class?

EXAMPLE: Listen to the teacher.
                Study your lesson.

_____

_____

_____

_____

 B. Ask your partner these questions:

1. What are the rules in this school?
2. Who makes the rules in our school?
3. Do you think more rules are needed?
4. How do adult students participate in making the rules at this school?

C. Work with your partner. Write two new rules for your school or for your class.

EXAMPLE: Keep the school clean.

_____

_____

_____

D. Read your ideas to your class.

2 Citizenship Reading

A. What do you know about these words? Write your ideas on the lines.

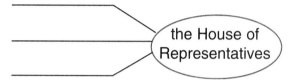

the House of Representatives   the Senate

B. Read

The Federal Government and Congress There are three branches of the U.S. government: the Legislative Branch, the Judicial Branch, and the Executive Branch.

The Legislative Branch This is the Congress. Congress makes the laws. There are two parts of Congress, the House of Representatives and the Senate.

Congress meets at the Capitol Building in Washington, D.C. All the members of the House of Representatives and the Senate are elected by the people. Citizens vote for the senators and representatives from their state.

The U. S. Capitol Building

The Senate There are 100 senators in Congress. Each state has two senators. Each senator is elected for a six-year term. A senator must be at least 30 years old and a U. S. citizen.

Senators can be re-elected. The leader of the Senate is the Vice President of the United States.

The House of Representatives   There are 435 members of the House of Representatives. The number of representatives a state has depends on how many people live in that state. A state with a large population has more representatives. A state with a small population has fewer representatives.

Each representative is elected for a two-year term. Representatives must be at least 25 years old and a U.S. citizen. They can be re-elected. The leader of the House of Representatives is called the Speaker of the House.

Powers of Congress   Congress has the power to: declare war, make laws, collect taxes, borrow money, control immigration, and set up a judicial and postal system. To make a law, first a bill passes the House of Representatives and the Senate. Then, the President signs the bill into law. If the President vetoes (rejects) the bill, the bill goes back to the Senate and the House to be voted on again. It must pass in the Senate and the House with a two-thirds majority vote. Then, the bill becomes a law.

C. Read the story again. Circle any new words. Add these words to your dictionary. Discuss the new words with your teacher and your class.

3 After You Read

A. Study the chart. Ask your partner four questions about the chart.

The Legislative Branch = The Congress		
	Senate	**House of Representatives**
How many?	100 Senators	435 Representatives
How long?	6 year term	2 year term
Age?	30 years old	25 years old
Leader?	Vice President	Speaker of the House

B. Read the sentences. Put a ✔ in the correct column. You may check more than one column.

	House of Representatives	Senate
1. There are 435 elected members.	✔	
2. The elected term is for six years.		
3. It is a part of Congress.		
4. Bills are passed there.		
5. The leader is the Vice President.		

C. Fill in the words. Read the story with a classmate.

laws   ~~Congress~~   Vice President

Senate   President   435

100   House of Representatives   Speaker

_____Congress_____ is the legislative branch of the U.S. government.

Congress makes the _____. The _____ and the

_____ _____ _____ are the two parts of Congress.

After a bill passes the House and Senate, the _____ must sign it.

There are _____ senators in the U.S. Senate. The

leader of the Senate is the _____ _____. There

are _____ members in the House of Representatives. The

leader of the House is the _____ of the House. Senators

and representatives can be re-elected.

Daniel Inouye

▽ 4 ▽ Make It Real

A. Talk about these questions with your teacher and your class:

1. The U.S. senators from this state are _____, and _____.

2. The U.S. representatives from this area are _____, and _____.

B. Sit in a group of four. Read the scenes below. Talk in your group about one scene.

SCENE 1 Imagine you are a U.S. Senator or U.S. Representative. There is a problem of violence in your area. You are writing a bill to control who can have or use a gun. Talk to the people from your area about how you feel. One group member writes the ideas.	**SCENE 2** Imagine you are a community member. You are at a neighborhood meeting. There are gang problems in your neighborhood and problems with guns. You think every person must protect herself or himself. Talk about how you feel. One group member writes the ideas.

C. Now, meet a student from the other group. Introduce yourself. Talk about neighborhood problems. Talk about a solution.

 5 Real Stories

A. Read a student's story

WHY I WANT TO BE AN ELECTED REPRESENTATIVE

Mohammad H. Chowdhury

I feel terrible when I see that crime rates are high in neighborhoods where poor people live, that kids are on drugs, youngsters are dropping out of school and becoming gang members, and that homeless people are on the street. As an elected representative, I will work with other Congress members to help poor people. Our government is spending billions for poor countries but not spending enough on its poor people. We need to take care of our poor people first. Charity always starts at home.

B. Talk to a classmate about this question:

Do you want to be an elected senator or a representative? Why or why not?

To be a good representative or senator you need to:
- Think about the problems in your community
- Talk to neighborhood people and get information
- Write and pass laws in Congress

C. Write about being an elected representative.

_____

_____

_____

_____

_____

D. Read your story to a partner. Ask your partner a question about his or her story.

▽ 6 ▽ Take the Test

(This section will give you practice for the citizenship test.)

A. Talk about the questions with a partner. Circle the correct answer. (Answers are at the bottom of the next page.)

1. What is the legislative branch of government?
   a. the President
   b. the Vice President
   c. the Congress
   d. the Judiciary

2. What is Congress?
   a. the Senate and the House of Representatives
   b. a state
   c. the Washington Monument
   d. the Lincoln Memorial

3. How many senators are there in Congress?
   a. 50
   b. 100
   c. 200
   d. 435

4. How many representatives are there in Congress?
   a. 50
   b. 100
   c. 200
   d. 435

B. Sit with a partner. Student A dictates sentences 1 and 2 to Student B. Then, Student B dictates sentences 3 and 4 to Student A. Check your sentences.

1. The Congress meets in the Capitol Building.
2. There are two (2) senators from each state.
3. The Congress makes the laws in the United States.
4. The Congress has two houses.

C. More Eligibility Questions: Interview your partner. (See pages 78 and 79 in Chapter 10 for additional questions.)

1. Have you filed a tax return for the last five years?
2. Have you ever been deported? If so, why do you want to be a citizen now?
3. Have you ever been a habitual drunkard?
4. Have you ever received income from illegal gambling?

▼▼▼▼▼▼▼▼▼▼▼▼▼▼▼▼▼▼▼▼▼▼▼▼▼▼▼▼▼▼▼▼▼▼▼

D. Clarification: If you don't understand something in the interview, you can say: *I'm sorry. Do you mean* _____ *or* _____?

7 ▽ Think About Your Learning

A. My favorite activity in this unit was _____.

I want to study more about:

▼ the Legislative Branch   ▼ the House of Representatives

▼ the Senate   ▼ _____
                                    (other)

Answers: 1.c 2.a 3.b 4.d

	Can a senator be re-elected?	What are four things Congress can do?	What are the three branches of government?	FINISH
Who is the leader of the House of Representatives?	Who is the leader of the Senate?	How long is one term in the House of Representatives?	How old must a representative be?	
Why are there 100 senators?	How long is one term in the Senate?		How old must a senator be?	How many representatives are there?
	How many senators are there?	How are senators and representatives chosen?	What does Congress do?	Where is the Capitol Building?
START	What is the Legislative Branch of government?	What are the two branches of Congress?	Where does Congress meet?	

The Executive and Judicial Branches

1 Before You Read

A. Sit in a group of four. Look at the pictures above. Talk about the questions. Write your answers in your book.

1. Who is the President of the United States? _____

2. What does the President do? _____

3. Who is the Vice President of the United States? _____

4. What does the Vice President do? _____

5. What other people advise the President? _____

6. What is the Supreme Court? _____

7. What does the Supreme Court do? _____

B. Read your answers to your class.

2 Citizenship Reading

A. What do you know about these words? Write your ideas on the lines.

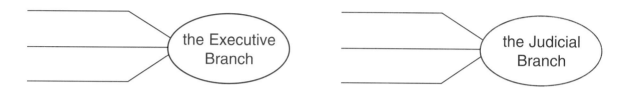

the Executive Branch

the Judicial Branch

B. Read

The Executive Branch   The Executive Branch enforces the laws passed by Congress. The President, the Vice President, and the Cabinet are the Executive Branch.

   The Central Intelligence Agency (CIA), the Federal Bureau of Investigation (FBI), the Environmental Protection Agency (EPA), and the Postal Service are some of the agencies in the Executive Branch.

The President and the Vice President   The President is the leader of the country. The President is also the leader of the Executive Branch. The President signs bills into law, enforces the law, prepares budgets, and is the Commander-in-Chief of the military. The President lives and works in the White House. The address of the White House is 1600 Pennsylvania Avenue, N.W., Washington, D.C. The Vice President helps the President and is the leader of the Senate.

   The President and the Vice President are each elected for a term of four years and can serve for two terms. We vote for the President and Vice President on General Election Day. It is the first Tuesday after the first Monday in November. In January, the President and Vice President are inaugurated (sworn into office).

General Information   To be President or Vice President, a person must be a natural born citizen of the United States, must be at least 35 years old, and must have lived in the United States for 14 years. If the President dies, the Vice President becomes the President. If the President and Vice President die, the Speaker of the House becomes the President. The President and Vice President are not directly elected by the people. The people vote for the Electoral College. The Electoral College members vote for the President and Vice President.

The Cabinet   The Cabinet advises the President. There are 13 Cabinet members. The Cabinet is appointed by the President. Some

Cabinet members are the Secretary of State, the Secretary of Defense, the Secretary of Commerce, the Secretary of Housing and Urban Development, and the Secretary of Education.

The Judicial Branch   The Judicial branch of the U.S. government includes the Supreme Court and the federal courts. The courts interpret (explain) the laws that the Legislative branch makes. The Supreme Court is the highest court in the United States. There are nine justices (judges) on the Supreme Court.

The nine justices are appointed by the President and ratified (approved) by Congress. The Chief Justice is the leader of the Supreme Court. The justices listen to the cases brought by the people. They decide the cases based on the Constitution and the laws of the United States. Supreme Court decisions are final.

C. Read the story again. Circle any new words. Add these words to your dictionary. Discuss the new words with your teacher and your class.

▽3▽ After You Read

A. Study the chart. Ask your partner the questions below.

The President and the Vice President	
How long?	4-year term
Age?	At least 35 years old
Birth?	Born a citizen of the United States
Terms?	Can be re-elected to a second term

B. Read the questions. Put a ✔ in the correct column.

	The Executive Branch (the President)	**The Judicial Branch** (the Justices)
1. Who lives and works in the White House?	✔	
2. Who interprets the Constitution and the laws?		
3. Who enforces the laws?		
4. Who is appointed by the President?		
5. Which branch is led by the Chief Justice?		

C. Fill in the words. Read the story with a classmate.

Electoral College	~~Executive~~	four	terms
Cabinet	November	Vice President	Supreme Court
President	interprets	nine	

The leader of the _____Executive_____ Branch is the _____.

The President is elected for _____ years. The President can

serve for two _____. Election Day is in _____.

Inauguration Day is in January.

The _____ _____ elects the President. The

_____ advises the President. If the President dies, the

_____ _____ becomes President.

The _____ _____ is the highest court in

the United States. The Supreme Court _____ the

Constitution and the laws. There are _____ Justices on the

Supreme Court.

4 ▽ Make It Real

A. Sit in a group of four. Read the scenes below. Talk in your group about one scene.

<table>
<tr><td>

SCENE 1

Imagine you are one of a group of senior citizens, over 65 years old. The people in your group are receiving money from Social Security, but it is not enough money to live on. Talk to the other people about how you feel. One group member writes the ideas.

</td><td>

SCENE 2

Imagine you are the President. There are many problems in your country: education, poverty, health care, and jobs. You want to help senior citizens live good lives, but there isn't sufficient money in the budget to give them more. Talk to your cabinet. One group member writes the ideas.

</td></tr>
</table>

B. Now, meet a student from the other group. Introduce yourself. Talk about the problems of getting older. Talk about federal budget problems.

5 ▽ Real Stories

A. Read a student's story.

Sandra Parada

THE EDUCATIONAL SYSTEM

I like the public educational system of the United States for several reasons. Students in high school don't have to pay for their classes. In the United States, students are provided with all the necessary books and materials they will use. For instance, when students are going to take a class such as government, they don't have to look for the book outside of school because they can get it from their own school. Also, the educational system helps students obtain knowledge in every subject they take. For example, students learn a lot by studying subjects such as health, economics, and government.

B. Talk to a classmate about this question:

Sandra wrote about the advantages of the educational system. What are some things you'd like to see improved in the educational system?

C. Write your opinion about the educational system.

_____

_____

_____

_____

_____

D. Read your story to a partner. Ask your partner a question about her or his story.

▽6▽ Take the Test

(This section will give you practice for the citizenship test.)

A. Talk about the questions with a partner. Circle the correct answer. (Answers are at the bottom of this page.)

1. What is the Executive Branch of our government?
   a. the President, Vice President, Cabinet, and departments
   b. the Capitol Building
   c. the Senate and the House of Representatives
   d. the Supreme Court

2. Who becomes President of the United States if the President should die?
   a. the Speaker of the House   b. the Vice President
   c. the past President   d. a Supreme Court Justice

3. How many Supreme Court Justices are there?
   a. six   b. twelve
   c. three   d. nine

4. What is the Judicial Branch of our government?
   a. the Congress   b. the President
   c. the Supreme Court   d. the Senate

Answers: 1. a   2. b   3. d   4. c

▼ ▼ ▼ **63**

B. Sit with a partner. Student A dictates sentences 1 and 2 to Student B. Then, Student B dictates sentences 3 and 4 to Student A. Check your sentences.

1. The President lives in the White House.
2. Washington, D.C. is the capital of the United States.
3. The President works in Washington, D.C.
4. _____ _____ is the President of the United States.

C. Allegiance to the United States Questions. Interview your partner. (See page 79 in Chapter 10 for additional questions.)

1. Do you believe in the Constitution and form of government of the United States?
2. Are you willing to take the Oath of Allegiance to the United States?
3. Are you willing to bear arms on behalf of the United States?
4. Are you willing to perform work of national importance under civilian direction?

▼ ▼

D. **Clarification:** If you don't understand something in the interview, you can say: *I'm sorry. I don't understand your question.*

7 Think About Your Learning

A. My favorite activity in this unit was _____ .
I want to study more about:

▼ the President   ▼ the Vice President

▼ the Cabinet   ▼ the Supreme Court

▼ _____
　　(other)

	What is the highest court of the United States?	How many justices are there on the Supreme Court?	How are the justices selected?	FINISH
Who becomes President when the President dies?	What is the address of the White House?	Where does the President live?	How many terms can the President serve?	
When do we vote for President?	When is the President inaugurated?		Name three requirements to be President.	How long is the President's term?
	Who is the Commander in Chief of the military?	What does the President do?	Which branch interprets the laws?	Which branch of government enforces the laws?
START	How many branches of government are there?	Name the three branches of government.	Which branch of government passes the laws?	

9 State and Local Government

1 Before You Read

A. Talk about these questions with your teacher and your class.
Fill in your answers.

State Geography and History	
1. What is the name of this state?	
2. Is this state in the North, South, East, West or middle of the United States?	
3. What is the capital of this state?	
State Government	
4. Who is the governor of this state?	
5. What are the legislative branches of this state?	
6. Who are the state senators or representatives from this area?	
7. What is the highest court in this state?	
Local Government	
8. Who is the mayor (chief executive) of this city?	
9. Is there a city council or city commission?	
10. Is there a county board of supervisors or county commission?	
11. Is there a city manager?	

B. Find out some other information about this state: the population, the year this state joined the Union, the state flower, and the state bird.

2 ⟁ Citizenship Reading

A. What do you know about these words? Write your ideas on the lines.

governor   mayor

B. Read

State Government		
Executive Branch	**Legislative Branch**	**Judicial Branch**
Governor	State senators and state representatives	State supreme court and lower state courts

State Government   Each of the 50 states has its own government and constitution. Like the federal government, each state government has three branches: the legislative, the executive, and the judicial. The chief executive of the state is the governor. The governor enforces state laws. The state legislature makes the state laws. State laws must agree with the U. S. Constitution. States make laws about work, school, property, and marriage. State senators, state representatives, and state government officials are elected by the people. States raise money from taxes. States provide services in education, welfare, roads, public health, jails, and regulation of businesses.

Local Government		
Executive Branch	**Legislative Branch**	**Judicial Branch**
Mayor or City Manager	City Council or County Commission	Municipal Court and Superior Court

Local Government — Towns, Cities, and Counties   The local governments in each area are different. The chief of your local government may be the mayor or the city manager. A city council or city commission may make the laws for your city. A county board of supervisors or county commission may make the laws for your county. City and county government provide public services. Libraries, schools, police, fire, trash pick up, parks, public transportation, and health care are some of the services provided.

▼ ▼ ▼ **67**

C. Read the story again. Circle any new words. Add these new words to your dictionary. Discuss the new words with your teacher and your class.

3 After You Read

A. Read the sentences. Put a ✔ in the correct column. You may check more than one column.

	Federal	State
1. The chief executive is the President.	✔	
2. The chief executive is the Governor.		
3. There are three branches of government: legislative, executive, and judicial.		
4. The constitution is the highest law.		
5. The capital is in Washington, D.C.		

B. Fill in the words. Read the story with a classmate.

judicial   mayor   legislative   education
constitution   governor   libraries   welfare
city council   trash

There are 50 states in the United States. Each state has a

constitution . Each state government has three branches, the

_____, executive, and _____ branches. The chief

executive of each state is the _____. Some services that

states provide are _____ and _____.

The chief executive of a local government may be the

_____. In some cities, a _____ _____

makes the laws for the residents. Some services provided by cities

are _____ pick up and _____.

4 Make It Real

A. Sit in a group of four. Read the scenes below. Talk in your group about one scene.

<table>
<tr><td>

SCENE 1

Imagine you are a citizen. In your community there are many poor, working people who do not have enough money for medical care. The public health clinics need more tax dollars to stay open. Go to a public meeting. Give your opinion about why you think more tax money must be used for public health programs.

</td><td>

SCENE 2

Imagine you are a state senator. The economy of your state is bad. Your state has lost a lot of tax money. Talk to the other senators on your committee. How can you find extra money to keep public health programs open?

</td></tr>
</table>

B. Now, meet a student from the other group. Introduce yourself. Talk about why all people need good public health care. Talk about tuberculosis, AIDS, and other illnesses. What can you do?

5 Real Stories

A. Read a student's story.

Giang Dinh

LIVING IN A NEW COUNTRY

I am a Vietnamese refugee. I've never forgotten my first feelings when I came to live in Canoga Park. Everything was very surprising and I felt lonely. I found out that people in the community saw me as a stranger. I was very sad. Images of my family and life in Vietnam returned to my mind. I tried to forget all my sad feelings because my children and I were living in a new country.

I had many new problems to think about. I had to study English and support my family. I had to adapt to the American community. Now, I am dreaming about my future as a citizen of the United States.

B. Talk to a classmate about this question:

1. Giang writes about his feelings of being in a new neighborhood and a new country. How did you feel about being in a new neighborhood and a new country?

C. Write about living in your neighborhood.

_____

_____

_____

_____

_____

D. Read your story to a partner. Ask your partner a question about her or his story.

▽ 6 ▽ Take the Test

(This section will give you practice for the citizenship test.)

A. Talk about the questions with a partner. Circle the correct answer. (Answers are at the bottom of this page.)

1. What is the head executive of a state government called?
   a. mayor   b. governor
   c. city manager   d. president

2. What is the head executive of a city called?
   a. mayor   b. governor
   c. judge   d. president

3. Who is the governor of our state?

   _____

4. Who is the chief executive of our local government?

   _____

B. Sit with a partner. Student A dictates sentences 1 and 2 to Student B. Then, Student B dictates sentences 3 and 4 to Student A. Check your sentences.

1. I live in _____, _____.
   city   *state*

2. The Vice President lives in Washington, D.C.

3. The mayor of this city is _____.

4. The governor of this state is _____.

C. Memberships and Organizations Questions. Interview your partner. (See page 79 in Chapter 10 for additional questions.)

1. What organizations and associations have you been part of in the United States?

2. How long have you been a member?

3. What kind of organization is it?

4. Where is the organization located?

▼ ▼

D. Clarification: If you don't understand something in the interview, you can say: *Excuse me. Did you say where? Or when?*

7 Think About Your Learning

A. My favorite activity in this unit was _____.

I want to study more about:

▼ State Government   ▼ Local Government

▼ _____
(other)

	What county do we live in? Spell it.	What is the name of this city/town? Spell it.	Is there a city council in our area?	**FINISH**
Who is the chief executive of our local government?		What is the highest court called in our state?	What is the legislature called in our state?	Name three services that a state provides.
Which branch of government makes state laws?	What does the governor do?		Who is the governor of our state?	How does our state raise money?
	Name the three branches of state government.	Does our state have its own government?	Does our state have its own constitution?	What is the abbreviation for our state?
START	What is our state's name? Spell it.	What is our state's capital? Spell it.	What year was our state admitted to the Union?	

Becoming a Citizen

1 Before You Read

A. Sit in a group of four. Look at the picture. Talk about the question. Write your answers.

What are some things a citizen of the United States can do?

vote for President _____ _____

_____ _____ _____

_____ _____ _____

B. Find out about your classmates. Fill in the chart.

Why do you think you will be a good citizen of the United States?

Name	Why
Chang	he goes to community meetings and tries to make things better

C. Read your ideas to your class.

> EXAMPLE: Chang will be a good citizen because he goes to community meetings and tries to make things better.

2 ▽ Citizenship Reading

A. What do you know about these words? Write your ideas on the lines.

United
States
Citizen

B. Read

Requirements to Become a Citizen	
Age	1. You must be 18 years old or older.
Residency	2. You must be a lawful, permanent resident for five years. **OR** 3. You must be a lawful, permanent resident for three years if your husband or wife has been a citizen for three years and you have been living with your spouse.
Literacy and **Knowledge**	4. You must understand, speak, read, and write simple English. (There are some exceptions.) 5. You must pass an examination of U.S. history and government based on the 100 Immigration and Naturalization Service (INS) questions. You must pass a short dictation test.
Loyalty	6. You must be willing to protect the United States.
Documents	7. You must file the N-400 form and other necessary documents, medical reports, fingerprints, and photographs with the INS.

Supervisor Gloria Molina and Councilwoman Jackie Goldberg discuss neighborhood problems

Responsibilities of Citizens
• Learn about political issues at local, state, and national levels.
• Register and vote.
• Become involved in community groups. Give your opinions.
• Respect the rights and opinions of other people.
• Be of good moral character.
• Pay taxes.
• Obey the laws.

Opportunities for Citizens
• Work with government agencies, law enforcement, and on jobs limited to citizens.
• Run for and be elected to government office.
• Leave and re-enter the United States without difficulty.
• Receive some financial aid and scholarships limited to U.S. citizens.
• Petition for relatives to come to live in the United States.
• Travel with a U.S. passport.
• Be a member of a jury.

C. Read the information again. Circle any new words. Add these words to your dictionary. Discuss the new words with your teacher and your class.

3 ▽ After You Read

A. Fill in the words. Read the story with a classmate.

history	~~18~~	write	questions	lawful
vote	taxes	obey	moral	N-400

You need to be _____18_____ years old to become a naturalized citizen of the United States. In general, you must be a _____ permanent resident for five years before you can be a citizen. You need to understand, speak, read, and _____ English.

The examination you will take is about U.S. _____ and government. There are 100 possible _____. You must fill out an INS document called the _____ form. You will be interviewed about the information on this form. A person applying for citizenship must be of good _____ character.

A citizen is responsible for paying _____. Also, a citizen must _____ the law. A citizen learns about the issues at a local, state, and national level. After that, a citizen can _____ responsibly in an election.

4 ▽ Make It Real

A. In your INS interview, you'll be asked to raise your right hand and swear that you are telling the truth. You'll say, "I do." Practice this with your teacher and your class.

B. Preparing for Your Interview: Practice answering these general questions with your teacher and classmates.

- How are you today?
- What colors are your clothes?
- How did you get here today?
- What are you wearing today?
- Tell me about the weather today.
- Who was your teacher in the citizenship program?

C. These are the additional questions for each chapter. Practice them with your teacher and classmates. (See the N-400 Form in the beginning of the book.)

- Walk around the classroom.
- Ask each student one question.
- Move to another student and ask a different question.

1. PERSONAL INFORMATION QUESTIONS
  a. What's your name?
  b. What's your address?
  c. What's your birth date?
  d. Where were you born?
  e. What's your Social Security number?
  f. What's your Alien Registration number?

2. ELIGIBILITY QUESTIONS
  a. Are you a permanent resident?
  b. How long have you been a permanent resident?
  c. When and where did you enter the United States?
  d. Of what country are you a citizen?
  e. Have you used any other names since you became a permanent resident?
  f. Are you single, married, divorced, or widowed?
  g. Can you speak, read, and write English?
  h. Have you ever been absent from the United States since you became a permanent resident?
  i. How many times have you left the country?
  j. When and why were you absent?
  k. How long were you absent?
  l. Were you absent for more than six months at any time?

- Sit in a group of three.
- Student A asks the first four questions.
- Student B asks the next four questions.
- Student C asks the final four questions.

- Sit with a partner.
- Student A is the applicant.
- Student B is the INS interviewer.
- Interview your partner.
- Then change roles.

3. RESIDENCE AND EMPLOYMENT QUESTIONS
  a. How long have you lived at your present address?
  b. Where did you live before?
  c. How long have you worked at your present job?
  d. What is your position?
  e. What did you do on your last job?
  f. How long did you work there?
  g. Why did you leave your last job?
  h. Who supports you?
  i. Who supports your children?
  j. Are you receiving welfare or any form of public or government assistance?

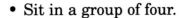

- Sit in a group of four.
- Each student selects three questions.
- Write each question on a separate piece of paper.
- Put the pieces of paper in a bag.
- Draw a question from the bag.
- Answer the question.

4. MARITAL HISTORY QUESTIONS

   a. Are you married now?
   b. How many times have you been married?
   c. What is the name of your husband or wife?
   d. What is his or her date of birth?
   e. Where was he or she born?
   f. What is his or her citizenship?
   g. What is his or her Social Security number?
   h. Is your wife or husband a naturalized citizen?
   i. What was the name of your previous spouse?
   j. How long were your married?

5. QUESTIONS ABOUT CHILDREN

   a. What is the name and age of your child (children)?
   b. What is the birth date of your child?
   c. Where was your child born?
   d. What country is your child a citizen of?
   e. What is your child's Alien Registration number?
   f. Where does your child live?
   g. Who supports your child?

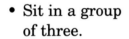

- Sit in a group of four.
- Study the questions.
- Answer one question.

   EXAMPLE: **My son was born on May 15, 1986.**

- The other students look at the list and find the correct question.

- Sit in a group of three.
- In each question circle key vocabulary words.
- Make a list of the words and discuss them.

6. and 7. MORE ELIGIBILITY QUESTIONS

   a. Have you ever been associated with the Communist Party?
   b. Were you connected with the Nazi government of Germany between 1933 and 1945?
   c. Have you ever persecuted another person because of race, religion, national origin, or political opinion?
   d. Have you ever left the United States to avoid the draft?
   e. What is your Selective Service number?
   f. When did you register with the Selective Service?
   g. Did you ever apply for exemption from military service? Why?
   h. Have you ever deserted from the military of the United States?
   i. Have you filed a tax return for the first five years? Did you ever fail to file your taxes after you became a permanent resident?

6. and 7. CONTINUED

    j. Have you ever been deported?

    k. If you have been deported, why do you want to be a citizen now?

    l. Have you ever claimed to be a U.S. citizen when you were not?

    m. Have you ever been a habitual drunkard?

    n. Have you ever advocated or practiced polygamy?

    o. Have you ever been a prostitute or procured anyone for prostitution?

    p. Have you ever helped anyone enter the country illegally?

    q. Have you ever received income for illegal gambling?

    r. Have you ever given false testimony to obtain an immigration benefit?

    s. Have you ever been a patient in a mental institution?

    t. Have you ever taken narcotic drugs?

    u. Have you ever committed a crime?

    v. Have you ever been arrested for or convicted of committing a crime? When? Where?

• Talk to your teacher and classmates about how you would answer these questions and why.

8. ALLEGIANCE TO THE UNITED STATES QUESTIONS

    a. Do you believe in the Constitution and the form of government of the United States?

    b. Are you willing to take the Oath of Allegiance to the United States?

    c. Are you willing to bear arms on behalf of the United States?

    d. Are you willing to perform noncombatant services in the Armed Forces?

    e. Are you willing to perform work of national importance under civilian direction?

9. MEMBERSHIPS AND ORGANIZATIONS QUESTIONS

    a. What organization or association have you been a part of in the United States?

    b. What kind of organization is it?

10. SIGNATURE

Do you affirm, under penalty of perjury, that all this information is true and correct?

Real Stories

A. Read a student's story

Hein Nhes

MY CITIZENSHIP INTERVIEW

Last week I had my citizenship interview and I passed! On the day of the interview, my American teacher came to help me. My heart was pounding and my hands were cold. The interviewer was friendly. He asked me questions about American government and history. I remember most of the questions: How many branches of government are there? How many senators? Who elects the President? Who was the first President?

One week after, I went back to my class to talk about the interview. I told the students, "Don't worry. You can pass the test, too. It's not too difficult!"

B. Talk to a classmate about these questions:

1. How did Hein feel on the day of her test?
2. How do you think you will feel on the day of your test?
3. What does it mean to you to be a citizen?

C. Write about becoming a citizen.

_____

_____

_____

_____

_____

_____

D. Read your story to a partner. Ask your partner a question about his or her story.

6 Take the Test

(This section will give you practice for the citizenship test.)

A. Talk about the questions with a partner. Circle the correct answer. (Answers are at the bottom of this page.)

1. What Immigration and Naturalization form is used to apply to become a naturalized citizen?
   - a. N-200
   - b. I-158
   - c. N-400
   - d. INS 303

2. What is the most important right granted to U.S. citizens?
   - a. the right to have a passport
   - b. the right to obey the law
   - c. the right to work
   - d. the right to vote

3. Name one benefit of being a citizen of the United States.
   - a. You can buy stamps.
   - b. You can travel with a U. S. passport.
   - c. You pay no taxes.
   - d. You can drive a car.

▼▼▼▼▼▼▼▼▼▼▼▼▼▼▼▼▼▼▼▼▼▼▼▼▼▼▼▼▼▼▼▼▼▼▼▼▼▼

B. **Clarification:** When someone asks you to sign the form, if you don't know where to sign, you can ask: *Where do I sign my name?*

7 Think About Your Learning

A. My favorite activity in this unit was _____ .

I want to study more about:

- ▼ Becoming a Citizen
- ▼ Rights and Responsibilities of Citizenship
- ▼ the INS Interview
- ▼ _____
  (other)

Answers: 1.c 2.d 3.b

Introduction to the Beginning Level Pages

The following 10 pages are designed to familiarize the beginning student with citizenship material.

Suggested Teaching Procedures:

1. The teacher sets the context with words and realia.

    EXAMPLE: Today we're going to talk about Thanksgiving. Do you know when Thanksgiving is?

    Teacher shows a picture of a turkey and a calendar with Thanksgiving circled.

2. The students look at the pictures on the page.

3. The teacher reads the sentences slowly to the class. The students look at the pictures again. Before reading each sentence, the teacher says the picture number.

    EXAMPLE: Picture 1—The Pilgrims leave England.
    Picture 2—They sail on the Mayflower.

    (This may be repeated several times)

4. The teacher reads the sentences again. Students point to the pictures.

5. The teacher says, "Point to the Pilgrims in Picture 1. Point to the Mayflower in Picture 2."

6. The teacher asks "What do you see in Picture 2? What do you see in Picture 3?"

7. The teacher reads the sentences with the students. (repeat)

To Focus on Listening

- The teacher pronounces words. Students point to the pictures.
- The teacher pronounces key words in random order. Students circle the words.

To Focus on Reading and Speaking

- Students practice reading the sentences with a classmate.
- A student points to the picture. A classmate reads the sentences.

To Focus on Writing

- Students copy the key words and sentences.
- Students practice spelling the words with a classmate.
- The teacher dictates the key words or sentences.

Chapter 1

A. Look at the pictures. Look at the words under the pictures.

1
- *Pilgrims*
- *England*
- *religious freedom*

2
- *sail*
- *Mayflower*

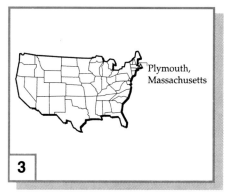

3
- *arrive*
- *Plymouth, Massachusetts*
- *1620*

4
- *Indians (Native Americans)*
- *teach*
- *plant, hunt, fish*

5
- *celebrate*
- *first Thanksgiving*

6
- *fourth Thursday*
- *November*

B. Look at the pictures again. Listen to your teacher read the sentences. Read with your class. Copy the sentences.

1. The Pilgrims leave England. They want religious freedom.
2. They sail on the Mayflower.
3. They arrive at Plymouth, Massachusetts in 1620.
4. Indians (Native Americans) teach the Pilgrims to plant, hunt, and fish.
5. The Pilgrims and the Indians (Native Americans) celebrate the first Thanksgiving.
6. Thanksgiving is the fourth Thursday in November.

Chapter 2

A. Look at the pictures. Look at the words under the pictures.

1

• 13 colonies

2

• English
• tax
• tea, sugar, stamps

3

• colonists
• Declaration of Independence
• 1776

4

• American Revolution
• 1783

5

• George Washington
• President

6

• July 4
• Independence Day

B. Look at the pictures again. Listen to your teacher read the
sentences. Read with your class. Copy the sentences.

1. There are 13 colonies.
2. The English tax tea, sugar, and stamps.
3. Colonists sign the Declaration of Independence in 1776.
4. The colonists win the American Revolution in 1783.
5. George Washington is the first President of the United
   States.
6. July 4 is Independence Day.

Chapter 3

A. Look at the pictures. Look at the words under the pictures.

1
- Constitution
- highest law

2
- Bill of Rights
- amendments

3
- freedom of speech
- say
- think

4
- freedom of assembly
- meet
- group

5
- freedom of religion
- practice
- religion

6
- freedom of press
- publish
- ideas

B. Look at the pictures again. Listen to your teacher read the sentences. Read with your class. Copy the sentences.

1. The Constitution is the highest law of the land.
2. The Bill of Rights is the first ten amendments to the Constitution.
3. Freedom of speech is the right to say what you think.
4. Freedom of assembly is the right to meet in a group.
5. Freedom of religion is the right to practice religion.
6. Freedom of press is the right to publish your ideas.

Chapter 4

A. Look at the pictures. Look at the words under the pictures.

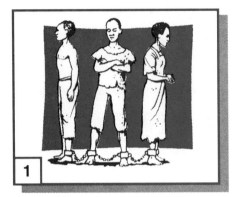

1
- *African slaves*
- *America*
- *chains*

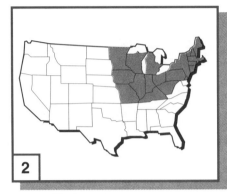

2
- *Northern states*
- *workers*
- *free*

3
- *Southern states*
- *slaves*

4
- *Abraham Lincoln*
- *President*
- *1861–1865*

5
- *soldiers*
- *Civil War*

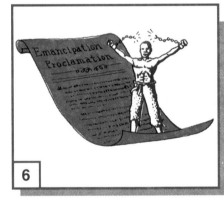

6
- *Emancipation Proclamation*
- *frees the slaves*

B. Look at the pictures again. Listen to your teacher read the sentences. Read with your class. Copy the sentences.

1. African slaves come to America in chains.
2. Northern states want workers to be free.
3. Southern states want slaves.
4. Abraham Lincoln is President from 1861 to 1865.
5. Northern soldiers win the Civil War.
6. The Emancipation Proclamation frees the slaves.

Chapter 5

A. Look at the pictures. Look at the words under the pictures.

1
- *workers*
- *better conditions*
- *1900*

2
- *World War I*
- *1914–1918*

3
- *women*
- *vote*
- *1920*

4
- *Depression*
- *no money*

5
- *World War II*
- *1939–1945*

6
- *Dr. Martin Luther King, Jr.*
- *equality*
- *1929–1968*

B. Look at the pictures again. Listen to your teacher read the sentences. Read with your class. Copy the sentences.

1. Workers want better working conditions in 1900.
2. World War I is from 1914 to 1918.
3. Women vote in 1920.
4. In the Depression people have no money.
5. World War II is from 1939 to 1945.
6. Dr. Martin Luther King, Jr. wants equality for all people. He lives from 1929 to 1968.

Chapter 6

A. Look at the pictures. Look at the words under the pictures.

1
- *flag*
- *United States*

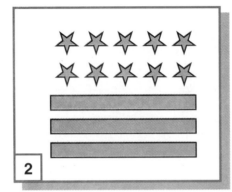

2
- *stars*
- *stripes*

3
- *June 14*
- *Flag Day*

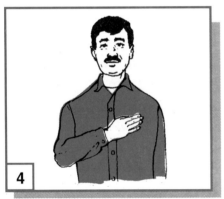

4
- *right hand*
- *heart*

5
- *pledge allegiance*
- *flag*

6
- *Star-Spangled Banner*
- *national song*

B. Look at the pictures again. Listen to your teacher read the sentences. Read with your class. Copy the sentences.

1. This is the flag of the United States.
2. There are 50 stars. There are 13 stripes.
3. June 14 is Flag Day.
4. Put your right hand over your heart.
5. Say, "I pledge allegiance to the flag . . ."
6. The Star Spangled Banner is the national song.

Chapter 7

A. Look at the pictures. Look at the words under the pictures.

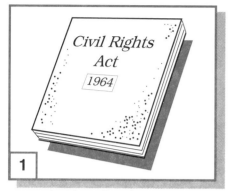

1
• Legislative Branch
• makes laws

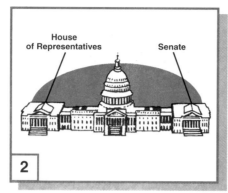

2
• Senate
• House of Representatives

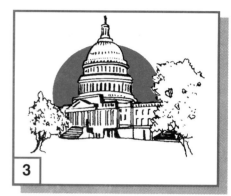

3
• Capitol Building
• Washington, D.C.

4
• 100
• Senators

5
• 435
• Representatives

6
• vote for
• Senators and Representatives

B. Look at the pictures again. Listen to your teacher read the sentences. Read with your class. Copy the sentences.

1. The Legislative Branch makes the laws.
2. The Senate and the House of Representatives are two parts of the Legislative Branch.
3. Members of the Senate and the House meet in the Capitol Building in Washington, D.C.
4. There are 100 senators.
5. There are 435 representatives.
6. We vote for senators and representatives.

Chapter 8

A. Look at the pictures. Look at the words under the pictures.

1

• *Election Day*
• *November*

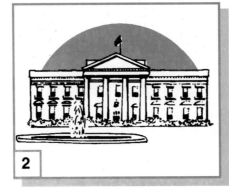

2

• *White House*

3

• *President*
• *can sign and veto laws*

4

• *leader*
• *country*

5

• *nine justices*
• *Supreme Court*

6

• *justices*
• *listen to*
• *decide court cases*

B. Look at the pictures again. Listen to your teacher read the sentences. Read with your class. Copy the sentences.

1. Election Day is in November.
2. The White House is where the President lives and works.
3. The President can sign and veto laws.
4. The President is the leader of the country.
5. There are nine justices on the Supreme Court.
6. The justices listen to and decide court cases.

Chapter 9

A. Listen to your teacher read. Copy the words. Read with your class.

An election of a local school board member

1. _____ is the name of this state.	**2.** _____ is the capital of this state.	**3.** _____ is the governor of this state.
4. She/he is a _____. (political party)	**5.** My state senator is _____.	**6.** She/he is a _____. (political party)
7. My state representative is _____.	**8.** He/she is a _____. (political party)	**9.** _____ is the name of this city.
10. _____ is the mayor/manager of this city.	**11.** She/he is a _____. (political party)	

B. Read the sentences with your class. Practice spelling the answers.

Chapter 10

A. Look at the pictures. Listen to your teacher read. Point to the pictures.

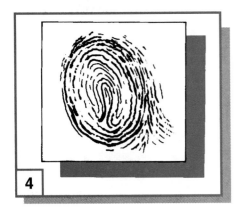

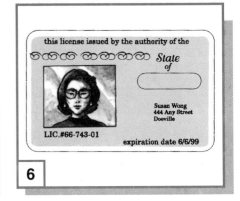

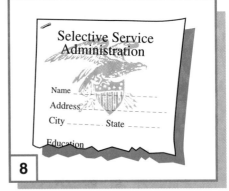

B. Look at the words. Listen to the teacher read the words. Match the words with the correct picture.

_____ Alien Registration card

_____ Marriage Certificate

_____ Social Security card

_____ Fingerprints

_____ Driver's License

_____ Selective Service papers

_____ Personal photos

_____ N-400 Form

100 Questions for Review

According to the INS, examiners are using these 100 questions, or questions similar to them, in their interviews of legalization applicants.

Test yourself. Cover the answers and try to answer the questions. Then practice asking and answering these questions with other students.

1. What are the colors of our flag?	Red, white, and blue
2. How many stars are there in our flag?	50
3. What color are the stars on our flag?	White
4. What do the stars on the flag mean?	One for each state in the union
5. How many stripes are there in the flag?	13
6. What color are the stripes?	Red and white
7. What do the stripes on the flag mean?	They represent the original 13 states
8. How many states are there in the Union?	50
9. What do we celebrate on the 4th of July?	Independence Day
10. What is the date of Independence Day?	July 4th
11. Independence from whom?	England
12. What country did we fight during the Revolutionary War?	England
13. Who was the first President of the United States?	George Washington
14. Who is the President of the United States today?	_____
15. Who is the Vice President of the United States?	_____
16. Who elects the President of the United States?	The Electoral College
17. Who becomes President of the United States if the President should die?	Vice President
18. For how long do we elect the President?	Four years
19. What is the Constitution?	The supreme law of the land
20. Can the Constitution be changed?	Yes
21. What do we call a change to the Constitution?	An amendment
22. How many changes or amendments are there to the Constitution?	27
23. How many branches are there in our government?	Three

24. What are the three branches of our government?

Legislative, Executive, and Judiciary

25. What is the Legislative Branch of our government?

Congress

26. Who makes the federal laws in the United States?

Congress

27. What is Congress?

The Senate and the House of Representatives

28. What are the duties of Congress?

To make laws

29. Who elects Congress?

The people

30. How many senators are there in Congress?

100

31. Can you name the two U.S. senators from your state?

_____

32. For how long do we elect each Senator?

Six years

33. How many voting members are in the House of Representatives?

435

34. For how long do we elect the representatives?

Two years

35. What is the Executive Branch of our government?

The President, cabinet, and departments under the cabinet members

36. What is the Judiciary Branch of our government?

The Supreme Court

37. What are the duties of the Supreme Court?

To interpret laws

38. What is the supreme law of the United States?

The Constitution

39. What is the Bill of Rights?

The first 10 amendments of the Constitution

40. What is the capital of your state?

_____

41. Who is the current governor of your state?

_____

42. Who becomes President of the United States if the President and the Vice President should die?

The Speaker of the House of Representatives

43. Who is the Chief Justice of the Supreme Court?

William Rehnquist

44. Can you name the 13 original states?

Connecticut, New Hampshire, New York, New Jersey, Massachusetts, Pennsylvania, Delaware, Virginia, North Carolina, South Carolina, Georgia, Rhode Island, and Maryland

45. Who said, "Give me liberty or give me death."?

Patrick Henry

46. Which countries were our enemies during World War II? — Germany, Italy, and Japan

47. What is the 49th state added to our Union (the United States)? — Alaska

48. How many full terms can a President serve? — Two

49. Who was Martin Luther King, Jr.? — A civil rights leader

50. Who is the head of your local government? — _____

51. According to the Constitution, a person must meet certain requirements in order to be eligible to become President. Name one of these requirements. — Must be a natural born citizen of the United States; Must be at least 35 years old by the time he/she will serve; Must have lived in the United States for at least 14 years.

52. Why are there 100 Senators in the Senate? — Because there are two from each state

53. Who nominates judges of the Supreme Court? — They are appointed by the President

54. How many Supreme Court justices are there? — Nine

55. Why did the Pilgrims come to America? — For religious freedom

56. What is the head executive of a state government called? — Governor

57. What is the head executive of a city government called? — Mayor

58. What holiday was celebrated for the first time by the American colonists? — Thanksgiving

59. Who was the main writer of the Declaration of Independence? — Thomas Jefferson

60. When was the Declaration of Independence adopted? — July 4, 1776

61. What is the basic belief of the Declaration of Independence? — That all men are created equal

62. What is the national anthem of the United States? — The Star-Spangled Banner

63. Who wrote the Star-Spangled Banner? — Francis Scott Key

64. Where does freedom of speech come from? — The Bill of Rights

65. What is the minimum voting age in the United States? — Eighteen

66. Who signs bills into law? — The President

67. What is the highest court in the United States? — The Supreme Court

68. Who was President during the Civil War?	Abraham Lincoln
69. What did the Emancipation Proclamation do?	It freed many slaves
70. What special group advises the President?	The Cabinet
71. Which President is called "the Father of Our Country"?	George Washington
72. What is the 50th state of the Union (the United States)?	Hawaii
73. Who helped the Pilgrims in America?	The American Indians (Native Americans)
74. What is the name of the ship that brought the Pilgrims to America?	The Mayflower
75. What were the 13 original states of the United States called?	Colonies

76. Name three rights or freedoms guaranteed by the Bill of Rights.

- The right of freedom of speech, press, religion, peaceable assembly and requesting change of government.
- The right to bear arms (the right to have weapons or own a gun, though subject to certain regulations).
- The government may not quarter, or house, soldiers in the people's homes during peacetime without the people's consent.
- The government may not search or take a person's property without a warrant.
- A person may not be tried twice for the same crime and does not have to testify against him/herself.
- A person charged with a crime still has some rights, such as the right to a trial and to have a lawyer.
- The right to trial by jury in most cases.
- Protects people against excessive or unreasonable fines or cruel and unusual punishment.
- The people have rights other than those mentioned in the Constitution.
- Any power not given to the federal government by the Constitution is a power of either the state or the people.

77. Who has the power to declare war?	The Congress
78. Name one amendment which guarantees or addresses voting rights.	Fifteenth, nineteenth, twenty-fourth, and twenty-sixth
79. Which President freed the slaves?	Abraham Lincoln

96 ▼ ▼ ▼

80. In what year was the Constitution written?	1787
81. What are the first 10 amendments to the Constitution called?	The Bill of Rights
82. Name one purpose of the United Nations.	For countries to discuss and try to resolve world problems; to provide economic aid to many countries.
83. Where does Congress meet?	In the Capitol Building in Washington, D.C.
84. Whose rights are guaranteed by the Constitution and the Bill of Rights?	Everyone (citizens and noncitizens living in the United States)
85. What is the introduction to the Constitution called?	The Preamble
86. Name one benefit of being a citizen of the United States.	Obtain federal government jobs; travel with a U.S. passport; petition for close relatives to come to the United States to live.
87. What is the most important right granted to U.S. citizens?	The right to vote
88. What is the United States Capitol (building)?	The place where Congress meets
89. What is the White House?	The President's official home
90. Where is the White House located?	Washington, D.C. (1600 Pennsylvania Avenue, N.W.)
91. What is the name of the President's official home?	The White House
92. Name one right guaranteed by the first amendment.	Freedom of: speech, press, religion, peaceable assembly, and requesting change of the government.
93. Who is the Commander-in-Chief of the U.S. military?	The President
94. Which President was the first Commander-in-Chief of the U.S. military?	George Washington
95. In what month do we vote for the President?	November
96. In what month is the new President inaugurated?	January
97. How many times may a Senator be re-elected?	There are no federal limits
98. How many times may a Congressman be re-elected?	There are no federal limits
99. What are the two major political parties in the United States today?	Democratic and Republican
100. How many states are there in the United States?	Fifty

▼ ▼ ▼ **97**

APPENDIX C Notes to the User

Below are suggestions for using and enhancing the activities in this book. Included are individual, pair, small group, and whole class activities.

1 Before You Read

Prereading activities provide learners the opportunity to activate prior knowledge and voice their opinions. Relying on their own experience and life skills, students generate words and ideas about the lesson theme in three general types of activities.

A. Discussing With a partner or in a small group, students ask and answer questions. Here is one way this can be done in a group: Student A asks Student B question #1. Student B answers. Student B asks Student C question #1. Student C answers. The same question is asked to all group members. The same procedure is used for the remaining questions.

B. Creating Charts Working with charts is a useful skill in academic and work-related environments. Students create charts using information they get from their peers. Students sit in groups of four. The teacher or the group selects a group leader. The leader asks the other three students the questions from the chart. One group member then asks the leader the questions.

C. Reporting Students share information and ideas with class. Listeners record new information in their books.

EXTENSION ACTIVITIES

• The teacher hangs large pieces of paper in different areas of the room and lists the words or ideas generated by the **Before You Read** section. Students write word associations on the paper with crayons or magic markers.

    EXAMPLE OF IDEA: **war**

    EXAMPLE OF WORD ASSOCIATIONS: **winning, death, soldiers.**

- As the groups report to the class, the teacher or a student creates a "class information" chart on the board. With the class information, students write sentences.

    EXAMPLE OF "CLASS INFORMATION": Twelve people from our class came to the United States by car.

- In groups of four, students write questions for ten minutes on the **Before You Read** topic. Then two groups work together. Each student asks someone from the other group questions.

2 Citizenship Reading

The short reading selections provide very specific citizenship information that is correlated to the INS questions.

A. **Thinking about Key Words** Two to three key words and ideas are presented in this section of each chapter. Together with classmates, students brainstorm word associations with the key words. With their teacher, they preview and predict the content material in the readings.

B. **Readings** After the word-association brainstorm, students discuss the subheadings and the pictures in each reading. The teacher reads a section to the class and then leads a discussion about it. Students may want to ask questions about the material, discuss vocabulary words in context, and then silently read the section. The teacher asks specific content-review questions.

C. **Creating a Student Dictionary** Students will come across new vocabulary words in each chapter. They can create a student dictionary for reference, using a notebook to record the words.

    As students re-read the text, they circle new vocabulary words. They then share these with the teacher who lists them on the board. The teacher explains each word, giving examples and a definition that students record in their dictionaries. Students then practice the definitions with one another.

    EXAMPLE: What is a <u>colony</u>?

    With a partner, students brainstorm and write a sentence to go with each word.

D. **Working with Timelines** The timelines can be used to review content information. Students ask each other *when* or *where* questions.

    EXAMPLE: When did the Pilgrims land at Plymouth, Massachusetts?

EXTENSION ACTIVITIES

- Learners write each event or date from the timeline on separate pieces of paper and put them in a bag. Each learner then draws a piece of paper and gives the date for an event or an event for a date.

- The teacher divides the class into two teams, writes events from the timeline on separate pieces of paper, and puts the papers in a bag. Students on one team draw papers from the bag and then line up in front of the class in correct chronological order. The other team acts as the judge.

- Students compare the timeline to events in their native countries during the same time period.

3 After You Read

Post-reading activities provide learners the opportunity to review and recycle the content material and vocabulary words. These encourage students to return to the reading to check for information. They also help students acquire essential information in a low-stress, high-success environment.

EXTENSION ACTIVITIES

- In pairs or small groups, students write *what*, *where*, *when*, *why*, and *how* questions about the information in the chapter. Using the questions, they quiz each other on the content.

- Students discuss historical events in their own countries and the events in each chapter: revolution, civil war, depression, etc.

4 Make It Real

Drama and role play can help bring the content of each chapter to life. Students form groups of four. Each group picks one of two scenes. Acting as the characters in the scene, learners discuss the issue for 15 minutes.) Representatives of the two groups meet to talk.

NOTE: Some students find it easier to role play than others. These questions can be asked by the teacher to assist students in the role play:

What do you think these people looked and dressed like at the time? What did they eat? What did they think about? What did they talk about?

5 Real Stories

Reading authentic student stories can stimulate learners to write their own personal stories. The following procedure is suggested.

A. Reading   Focusing on the photograph of the student writer and the story title, students predict what the story is about. Then they read the story and tell a partner what they liked about it.

B. Discussing and Writing   With a partner, students talk about the guided questions. These questions are intended to connect the story to students' personal experiences. After a discussion, students are ready to write their own personal stories. Finally, each student reads his or her story to a partner, and the partner asks a question about the story.

EXTENSION ACTIVITIES

- Learners work cooperatively in pairs to revise their personal stories.
- Learners make a class book of student writing for each topic. The books become "anthologies" for the class.

6 Take the Test

These activities prepare students for the citizenship test and the INS interview by giving them practice with the specific questions that may be asked. Multiple-choice, dictation, and interview questions are included. The **Clarification Section** helps students to request, with confidence, repetition and clarification of information during the interview.

7 Think About Your Learning

Students reflect on and begin taking responsibility for their learning by choosing their favorite activity and circling what they want to study more about.

Game

Reviewing the chapter content in a playful, non-threatening situation will help students internalize key facts. For this activity, each group of four will need a die and the game board from the unit, and each student will need a marker (a coin, a paper clip, or a pencil eraser). Students throw the die, move their markers around the game board, answer the questions they land on, and review the material in the chapter. If a student does not know the answer to a question, he or she goes back to their previous square. If a student lands on a picture square, no question is asked and he or she remains there until the next turn. The teacher facilitates the game by answering questions and settling disputes.

After all the groups have played the game once and are familiar with the questions and answers, two students from each group move to a different group and the new groups play the game again.

A Final Note

The information in this book is written to assist students in preparing for the naturalization process. While the N-400 Form is included here for reference, teachers should not use it or the contents of this book to provide legal advice to students. Legal advice about immigration must be obtained from qualified legal professionals.

To Minnie and Sam Hutton, Anna and Abram Magy, and Helen Rachinsky who shared their immigrant experiences with me.

To my editors, Roseanne Mendoza and Sally Conover, who saw me though this process, and to the following faculty and staff:

Joanne Abing, Steven Barba, Raquel Bautista, and Mim Paggi
South Gate Community Adult School

Pat Burns and Melinda Marley   Evans Community Adult School

Beth Easter   Adult Literacy Program Minneapolis Public School

Mayra Fernandez   Roosevelt Community Adult School

Afra Nobay   Los Angeles Community Adult School

Marna Shulberg   Van Nuys Community Adult School

Elsa Zamora   Los Angeles Unified School District.

To the reviewers for their insightful comments, and to Naomi Huerta for her wonderful photos.

A special thank you to Eva, Jackie, Linda, Frances, Barbara, and Inez for all their understanding and support.